ADVANCE PRAISE

An illuminating view of how school attendance zone policies all too often reinforce the disparity associated with housing inequality. A must-read for education leaders, policy makers, parents, and anyone who believes that a child's zip code should not prevent him or her from accessing the best education that a school district offers.

— TONY MILLER
former Deputy Secretary of Education under President Obama

Tim DeRoche offers a searing indictment of the way educational opportunity is distributed in America. Whether you agree or disagree with his particular solutions, DeRoche makes a powerful case that we must tear down the walls that exclude disadvantaged children from high-performing schools.

— RICHARD D. KAHLENBERG
senior fellow, The Century Foundation

An invaluable resource for parents. *A Fine Line* provides a thorough analysis of zip-code laws for every state, exposing the Education Apartheid that continues sixty-six years after the landmark *Brown v. Board of Education* Supreme Court case. DeRoche engages parents and gives them a voice in the vacuum that is education policy. There is no denying that schools attended by black and Hispanic students are under-funded and under-performing. Zip-code laws continue the injustice of Jim Crow laws. These laws condemn students to schools that have failed to educate communities for generations. This book allows readers to educate themselves on the discrimination and "redlining" that children in the education system experience. Every child deserves equal access to a high-quality education.

— MONA DAVIDS
founder and president of the New York City Parents Union

A Fine Line is a brilliant exposé of so-called "zip-code schools," a foundational weakness in our system of public education so profound that even *Brown v. Board of Education* could not make it right. Residential assignment of schools serves the state's interest in obliquely aligning with the most basic of state constitutional requirements to provide public education, but it divides us by race, income, and culture and does not serve the educational needs of children. Tim DeRoche deftly explains this, with clear data and sound reasoning. Is the purpose of public education to divide our children, put them in boxes dictated by arbitrary boundaries and call them equal? Or is the purpose of public education to provide genuine, publicly funded options for learning where children can thrive and be successful? Parents, not bureaucrats, deserve this right to choose the option best suited for their children. If you could redesign our system of public education, how would you do it? *A Fine Line* shows us where to begin.

– LESLIE HINER
vice president of legal affairs, EdChoice

The public-school system is supposed to be society's great equalizer. In theory, access to a public education is supposed to help the least advantaged gain the skills necessary to achieve the American Dream. In practice, as Tim DeRoche points out, the traditional public-school system actually exacerbates the inequities it was meant to cure. A child's school, and their future, depends on their zip code. But it doesn't have to be that way.

– COREY DeANGELIS
director of school choice, Reason Foundation

This is a rigorous account of why our schools are still separate and still unequal—even six decades after *Brown v. Board of Education*. DeRoche digs up the little-known laws and policies that dictate which kids are allowed to attend the best public schools—and who is left on the outside looking in. DeRoche asks the right question—what do we mean when we say that a school is "public"? This book will likely make you angry, but it also holds out the hope that one day even the best public schools will be open to everyone.

GREGORY McGINITY
former executive director of the Broad Foundation

A FINE LINE

A FINE LINE

HOW MOST AMERICAN KIDS ARE
KEPT OUT OF THE BEST PUBLIC SCHOOLS

TIM DeROCHE

Afterword by

GLORIA ROMERO

REDTAIL PRESS

REDTAIL PRESS

Published by Redtail Press
Los Angeles, California
www.redtailpress.com

**Library of Congress Cataloging-in-Publication
Data in progress**
DeRoche, Tim
ISBN 978-0-9992776-2-1 (hardcover)
Nonfiction

Photos of children and Tim DeRoche headshot by Kessia Embry
Book layout and design by Daniel González
Printed in the United States of America

First edition
1 2 3 4 5 6 7 8 9 0

For three educators...

Laura DeRoche
Ed DeRoche
Stacy Brock McLellan

CONTENTS

NEIGHBORHOOD POOLS

You wipe the sweat from your brow. It's Memorial Day, only the beginning of the summer, but the sun is already beating down at 9:30 a.m. You'd like to be out in the sunshine, but it's just too much. You tell your six-year-old daughter that she'd better just stay inside and play board games in the comfort of the AC.

But wait—there's good news! Your neighbor says that they're opening a brand-new, state-of-the-art pool at one of the local community centers, the first in over a decade. And today is the grand opening.

So you pack your daughter up in the Toyota and drive three short miles to a nearby neighborhood. A giant rainbow of balloons arches over the entrance to the pool. Kids are already streaming into the new facility. You have to park four blocks down, but your daughter doesn't mind a bit of a walk. The cool, clean water is beckoning. As you approach, you can hear kids yelling and laughing and splashing. Your daughter starts skipping, unable to contain her excitement.

You approach the gate and get in line with a bunch of other families. There's a man from the city there, and he asks to see your driver's license. "I'm sorry, ma'am," he says, handing it back to you. "We're not going to be able to let you in right away." He waves a couple of other families through.

Wait, what? Why?

He explains that your address doesn't fall within the "preference zone" for pool admission. This is a neighborhood pool, he says, and spots are reserved for the families in the immediate neighborhood.

A Mercedes pulls up, and four kids scamper out. The man waves them through. Your daughter starts to cry.

"You're welcome to wait in that line over there," he says and points to a long line snaking along the fence on the other side of the entrance. "If there's room, we may let in some kids from outside the neighborhood."

Hundreds of kids are lined up along the fence staring with forlorn faces through the links, watching the other kids play in the water. It's a disappointment, but you don't want to cause a fuss. It's not that big of a deal.

"C'mon, honey," you say to your daughter, gathering her into your arms. "Let's get in line. We'll just have to wait a little bit." The man from the city makes eye contact with you, and his eyes seem to say, "Don't get your hopes up."

As you're walking along the fence, you and your daughter get your first full view of the new facility. The main pool is Olympic sized, with gleaming white tile that shines in the sun. There's a kiddie pool and a splash pad, too. Dozens and dozens of kids are in there, jumping, splashing, diving. There's even a two-story waterslide. Muffled screams of joy echo from inside the giant yellow tube.

Smiling parents hang back on beach chairs scattered around the outskirts. A couple of them slather sunscreen on reluctant kids. It's the early summer, and everyone seems to be lily-white, ripe for the first sunburn of the year.

Then, as you turn the corner and take your place in the long line, you notice something. The kids in the long line along the fence are not lily-white. In fact, many of the waiting kids are dark skinned. Black and Hispanic. You hear an accent, a foreign phrase. Many of these kids speak English as a second language.

Something bubbles up inside you. Anger.

You march straight back up to the man at the gate. "I want to talk to someone," you say, and he points you over to a man who's being interviewed by a camera crew from the local TV news: It's your city councilman.

You get there just in time to hear him finish his interview. "We're just so pleased to be able to offer this type of facility to the community, a place where all the people of our community can gather together. This shows that government can work for the people of our city." He puts on a big smile and shakes the reporter's hand.

"Excuse me," you say. And you tell him your story. This can't be the best way to do it. This looks like discrimination. It looks like the city is trying to limit access to the pool to the wealthy and the privileged.

"No," he says. "We're just trying to make sure the pool isn't overrun by kids from outside the neighborhood."

But how was the pool paid for? "Out of the city's General Fund."

"I'm a resident of the city," you tell him. "I live just three miles away. You're my city councilman. And I pay taxes into that General Fund, so it's only fair my daughter have equal access to this pool."

"I'm sorry," he says. "We have a policy of building neighborhood pools. You have a pool in your neighborhood, don't you? Why don't you go back to that pool?"

You explain to him that you do indeed have a neighborhood pool. Unfortunately, it was built over one hundred years ago, and the city hasn't maintained it very well. The water has grown green with algae, and the tile is broken in many places, creating a tripping hazard. And there's no security. Your daughter had her scooter stolen from that park last year. What's more, because of the condition of the pool, they can't get experienced lifeguards to work there. One little boy almost drowned last year because the lifeguard service was so poor.

"I'm sorry to hear that," he says. "I'm sure the city will get to your pool eventually. We've got a budget crunch right now, but I'll bet that your pool is upgraded in the next decade or so. Then they'll be able to hire more experienced lifeguards."

"But my daughter is six!" you say. "We tried to buy a house in this neighborhood last year, but it was $200,000 more. Our family can't afford that."

"I'm sorry," he says. "I have to go join my family. I can assure you that this is the best possible system. The whole reason it's set up this way is so that poor kids have access to public pools."

The man at the gate smiles as he makes room for the councilman to slide past.

"Do you even live in this neighborhood?" you ask him through the fence.

"That's not relevant," he tells you. "I'm here on official city business." And then he walks away. Through the fence, you see him take off his shirt and take a running leap into the pool.

KER-SPLASH!

PREFACE

This book got its start back in 2013, when I was first introduced to Gloria Romero, the former majority leader of the California State Senate. At the time, Gloria was the head of the California chapter of Democrats for Education Reform (DFER) and was looking for someone who could help her with her efforts to increase educational options for poor kids in California.

Gloria and I met for coffee in the El Sereno neighborhood of Los Angeles, a predominantly Latino area that Gloria had represented for eight years in the state Senate. We quickly hit it off. We both shared a sense that American public education was failing our children. While in the Senate, Gloria had fought to empower parents with more control over their children's education, passing the famous "parent trigger" law that allowed parents to take control of a failing public school. She also passed the Romero Open Enrollment Act of 2010, which gave parents many more public-school choices for their kids, if their kids were assigned to a chronically failing school.

But Gloria didn't want to celebrate past legislative victories. She wanted to talk about other ways we could improve public schools for poor children. The key, she told me that afternoon, was breaking the link between your zip code and where you went to school.

Around the same time, Gloria gave a talk to the students of Whittier Law School in which she expanded on this idea:

Throughout the nation, school assignment is largely based on zip code—a geographic boundary. Five simple, arbitrary digits become the basis of separation from the American Dream for millions of children who, through no fault of their own, happen to live on one side of the tracks or the other. I ask you, where else in American life do we restrict opportunity and movement to geography? We have struck down racially restricted covenants in the purchase of homes, and we can move into any neighborhood. We can choose to worship at the church or temple of [our] choice. Imagine if you tried to visit a park and were asked for your papers at the entrance to the park and were informed, based on your zip code, that you could not enter because you were from the wrong side of town. Imagine if you could only choose to visit a dentist or a doctor or shop at a mall in "your neighborhood." We wouldn't stand for it. So why do we do this in education?[1]

I had been working in K–12 education reform, off and on, for over twenty years at that point. As a strategy and operations consultant, I have led projects for large public-school systems like the Los Angeles Unified School District, as well as for large nonprofits that operate charter schools. I've also served organizations focused on educational justice, like Education Trust–West, and policy advocates, like DFER.

From those twenty years of experience, I knew the outlines of the problem very well. In every large public district, there are chronically failing schools, and there are high-performing schools. The failing schools are typically clustered in low-income neighborhoods often serving mainly Hispanic and African American kids, while the high-performing schools are typically located in wealthier areas of the city and serve more white and Asian families.

On that day in El Sereno, I knew that the best public schools had no open seats, because so many parents want their kids to go to those schools. My friends in Los Angeles were often willing to pay a significant premium to live within the "attendance zone" for a high-performing school like Ivanhoe Elementary in the hilly and charming neighborhood of Silver Lake just a few miles from Downtown Los Angeles. Living in the Ivanhoe zone can run $200,000 extra for a home or up to $1,000 a month in extra rent.

I was vaguely aware that there are "open enrollment" laws on the books designed to allow poor children to escape failing schools and apply to higher-performing schools outside their neighborhood. But it didn't seem as though that happened very often.

Over coffee that day, I remember asking Gloria, "How do they keep those good schools so exclusive? How can the law allow that? They're *public* schools."

Gloria didn't know either.

So I started looking into it. What is the legal basis for keeping the best public schools reserved for those who pay for the right to live within the attendance zone? How is the school district able to do that lawfully? It seems like a clear violation of our right to be treated equally under the law. And it seems to defy the whole premise that public education can level the playing field for those born with less money and fewer advantages.

It was the start of a five-year trip down a rabbit hole of school-district admissions policies and state laws that govern student assignment in public-school systems. What I found astonished me. State laws are indeed being used to keep not just poor kids but *most* American kids of every ethnicity from attending elite public schools. These little-known laws perpetuate and even exacerbate the social divisions that have diminished our ability to move forward together as Americans.

I want to take you into a world in which private detectives secretly follow and use telephoto lenses to snap pictures of small children suspected of illegally attending a better school. This is a world in which nameless bureaucrats draw lines through our communities that sort kindergartners into winners and losers. A world in which parents are encouraged to use anonymous tip lines to turn in families they suspect of living outside the neighborhood. A world in which other parents are arrested and shamed for using a false address to get their child out of a failing school and into a better public school.

It's also a world in which district officials conduct "home checks" on homeless families, kicking their kids out of school if the family's car or tent is located in the wrong school zone.

This is a world governed by an unseen matrix of state laws and district policies that distort Americans' choices about education and real estate. Because of these rules, families of all income levels are forced to make gut-wrenching decisions about where to live and how to get their kids into better schools. Meanwhile, the media's coverage of the education wars focuses on the reliable clickbait of charter schools, teacher pay, and high-stakes testing.

The premise of this book is simple: If a child lives within the school district, it is morally wrong for that child—black or white, rich or poor— to be kept out of a district school because she lives on the wrong side of a line drawn by the district. Attendance-zone boundaries benefit a very small group of public-school parents who pay a pretty penny for privileged access to these elite schools. Public education would simply work better if our laws *forbade* districts from drawing these lines, rather than allowing them or even requiring them to do so.

I also outline how such laws and policies appear to violate constitutional protections, both state and federal, that are meant to ensure that public services are equally available to all citizens. And I discuss several different strategies—both legislative and judicial—that could be used to open up the public schools to all students on an equal basis.

My goal is to illuminate how these obscure laws provide the foundation for the failures and inequalities of our K–12 education system. I also want to suggest ways that we might bring public-school admissions policies into alignment with the principle of equal access that is so important for the social compact.

Someone may tell you that they know how to fix our system of public education. They may say that the solution is more funding, higher teacher pay, and smaller class sizes. Or they may argue that the answer is charter schools. Or tax credits that allow everyone to attend private schools.

You should be extremely skeptical of such easy answers. There are no panaceas for the ills of our public education system. No easy fixes. Decades of segregation and inequality, both deliberate and accidental, cannot be overcome with any single policy change.

But we must be wary of laws and policies that dictate who can or cannot attend schools meant for the public. Such laws and policies are particularly vulnerable to being co-opted by politically powerful interest groups that hope to capture public resources for themselves.

Access is the forgotten issue in K–12 education. Contrary to popular opinion, *Brown v. Board of Education* did not open up the public schools to everyone. Millions of children of all races are still excluded from the best public schools in their communities.

This book calls attention to those laws and policies that prevent most American kids from having equal access to the best public schools. These laws and policies are inconsistent with the values we hold dear as Americans.

They betray the American promise of public education.

LIST OF FIGURES AND TABLES

LIST OF FIGURES AND TABLES

Attendance zone maps in Appendix A

PART I: SEPARATED BY LAW

Chapter 1

The Promise of Public Education

Public education is a promise. It's a promise made by your state government to you. Every single state has a provision in its constitution that requires the state legislature to provide for public education.

It didn't have to be that way. The federal government makes no such promise, and the Supreme Court has ruled that there is no right to an education under the US Constitution (*San Antonio Independent School District v. Rodriguez*, 1973). But each of the fifty states does make this promise.

What is the nature of their commitment to us?

It differs by state. Minnesota uses utilitarian language in instructing the legislature to establish a "uniform system of public schools" and further requires that they be "thorough and efficient."[1] Arkansas is a bit more high-minded:

> Intelligence and virtue being the safeguards of liberty
> and the bulwark of a free and good government, the
> State shall ever maintain a general, suitable and effi-
> cient system of free public schools and shall adopt all
> suitable means to secure to the people the advantages
> and opportunities of education.[2]

Florida flings adjectives at the legislature, describing the anticipated system of public schools as "uniform, efficient, safe, secure, and high quality."[3]

Some states refer to "free public schools"; others call for a system of "common schools." Many require that the schools be nonsectarian; others do not. Some direct the legislature to fund the schools out of the general fund, while others leave the funding to local school districts or municipalities.

Although the specifics vary quite a bit from state to state, these constitutional promises are generally a reflection of the goals of the Common School Movement started by Horace Mann of Massachusetts in the 1800s. Mann, the great champion of universal public education, believed that education was the engine of democracy and that it would serve to put all citizens on an equal playing field, regardless of economic advantage. "Education then, beyond all other devices of human origin," Mann famously wrote, "is the great equalizer of the conditions of men, the balance-wheel of the social machinery."[4]

Many states adopted language inspired by Mann and his fellow champions of the common schools. You can hear it in Arkansas's declaration that "intelligence and virtue" are "the safeguards of liberty and the bulwark of a free and good government." Public schools, then, are the vehicle through which even the poorest citizen can become educated and contribute in a meaningful way to our democracy.

In recent years, many state courts have ruled that education is a "fundamental right" or "fundamental interest" under their respective state constitutions. This got its start in 1971 with the landmark case of *Serrano v. Priest* in California, which invalidated the state's funding system because it resulted in vast discrepancies in per-pupil spending between wealthy and poor districts. In *Serrano*, the California Supreme Court stated, "We are convinced that the distinctive and priceless function of education in our society warrants, indeed compels, our treating it as a 'fundamental interest.'"[5]

This ruling is partially justified by the explicit mention of education in the California Constitution. Because education is not mentioned in the US Constitution, federal courts have declined to rule that it is a fundamental right for all US residents. But the California determination in *Serrano* also springs from the California court's "recognition of the importance of education to our democratic society."[6]

This judgment that education is a fundamental right, now recognized by thirteen states,[7] is extremely important in the judicial context, because fundamental rights require strict enforcement of "the equal protection of the law," which is guaranteed by the Fourteenth Amendment.

In many states, the state constitution provides additional assurances meant to safeguard the public schools as truly public institutions. In these states the public schools must be "open to all" (Arizona, South Carolina, and several others) or "equally open to all" (Indiana). A handful of states even promise some variation of "equality of educational opportunity," including Louisiana, Montana, and North Carolina.[8]

The specificity of these provisions carries significant weight, because the school systems are public entities and governed democratically, either by elected or appointed officials. There is always a risk that a majority of voters will co-opt educational policy to benefit themselves rather than the public at large.

It's easiest to see this phenomenon when it is racially motivated.

The state of Alabama passed its constitution in 1901 with a promise of "a liberal system of public schools throughout the state." It added, however, an additional provision requiring separate schools for white and black children and specifying that "no child of either race shall be permitted to attend a school of the other race."[9] With that one clause, white citizens used the law, indeed the state constitution itself, to capture their neighborhood schools and exclude black children from attending. Other state legislatures passed statutes that accomplished the same thing, empowering districts to keep black or Hispanic or Asian kids out of the schools. California passed a law stating that "Negroes, Mongolians and Indians shall not be allowed into public schools."[10]

Of course, such segregation, whether created by state law or by school-district policy, was eventually outlawed in 1954 by the famous

Supreme Court ruling in *Brown v. Board of Education* that students could not be excluded from schools on the basis of race. Specifically, the court ruled that such policies are a violation of the Equal Protection Clause of the Fourteenth Amendment,[11] which was passed after the Civil War to ensure that the states would treat all people equally under the law.

Alabama, out of either indifference or incompetence or both, has never bothered to change the language in its 1901 constitution. The segregation clause remains, standing as a textual reminder of the ongoing danger that politicians will use the law to reserve some of the public schools for those with political power, while excluding the less advantaged.

History, then, would suggest that we should be vigilant about our educational laws and policies, especially as they dictate who can or cannot attend any given "public" school. Do student assignment policies live up to the promise of public education? Do they enable schools to be "open to all" children? Are they constructed in a way that allows the public schools to be an equalizing force? Or do these policies allow politically powerful special interests to take nominally public schools and make them exclusive or even—in effect—private?

These questions are especially apt in a world in which the quality of public schools is so variable, where your education—and therefore much of your life—turns on the simple fact of whether you live on the right or the wrong side of North Avenue.

Chapter 2

The Two Sides of North Avenue

_____

Residents of the Old Town neighborhood in Chicago cross busy North Avenue every day. If you live north of North, you might cross the street to grab a Happy Meal for your son at the local McDonald's. Or maybe you'd meet a friend for a pint at the Old Town Ale House, which is on the southeastern corner of Wieland and North.

If you live to the south, you might cross North Avenue to see a show at the world-famous Second City comedy club or to grab a bite at the Sedgwick Stop gastropub. Or maybe you pass North Avenue every Sunday when you take your family to the 11 a.m. choir service at St. Michael's Catholic Church, which is just one block north of North on Cleveland.

If you need medical care in Old Town, no matter which side of North Avenue you live on, you have your choice of Family Urgent Care on the north or Physicians Immediate Care on the south. Both receive excellent ratings from patients, 4.8 and 4.6 stars on Google Maps.[1]

Like many neighborhoods in America, there is no official definition of Old Town, no legal entity that can claim that name. But the former art critic for the *Chicago Tribune* Alan G. Artner, who lives in the neighborhood, once wrote, "This neighborhood is supposed to be as much a sound as a place, and it's from the bells of St. Michael's Church. The story goes you only really live in Old Town if you can hear them."[2]

Old Town has become one of the most attractive neighborhoods on the North Side of Chicago, just a couple of miles from downtown. The streets are lined with trees and townhomes, many of the units having been built in the first half of the twentieth century, but also some that have gone up in one of the two housing booms since 2000. Drugstores and grocery markets and pubs and gyms—all are within walking distance of the neighborhood's main drag, North Avenue. And the Brown Line of the "el" train cuts right through the neighborhood on a diagonal, dropping passengers off just a block south of North Avenue at the Sedgwick station.

Nothing about North Avenue in Old Town feels like a political barrier or a sociological fault line. But that's what it is. In one extremely important way.

If you stand in front of the recently closed Marcello's Restaurant at the corner of Larrabee and North, there are two public elementary schools within a mile. Both schools are operated by the Chicago Public Schools. Both are governed by the decisions of the Board of Education. Both are funded by Chicago residents, who pay property taxes directly into the Chicago Public Schools General Fund. So residents living north and south of North Avenue share the burden of funding the two schools.

But neighborhood families do not share equal access to the two local schools. When it comes to public education, North Avenue separates the residents of Old Town into two very different groups.

Let's look at the two schools.

Turn north on Larrabee Street and walk seven blocks to Lincoln Elementary School, one of the crown jewels of the Chicago Public Schools. Lincoln gets a "1+" rating from the district, the highest possible rating.[3] And the school operates the prestigious French-American School of Chicago, officially recognized by the French Ministry of Education and open only to students of Lincoln Elementary. Here's how Lincoln Elementary describes itself:

> The Lincoln School is recognized as a model school
> within the Chicago Public Schools. We set the highest
> standards for our students in academic achievement,
> intellectual growth and rigor, ethical awareness and

behavior, and exceptional sportsmanship. Our balance
of tradition and innovation continue to provide excellent opportunities to deserving students from diverse
social, ethnic, and socio-economic backgrounds.
Come join the traditions we hold true and experience
the best in public education.[4]

Now walk back to Larrabee and North. Turn south this time, and walk
five blocks to Manierre Elementary School. Manierre receives a "3" rating
from the district, the lowest possible rating. It probably doesn't surprise
you that Manierre's performance falls short of Lincoln's. Most public
schools fall short of the Lincoln standard. But Manierre doesn't just lag
Lincoln. Manierre, by any objective standard, is a failing school.

Compare the reading proficiency of students at the two schools: At
Lincoln, 80% of students are proficient in reading for their grade level,
compared to 11% at Manierre. The state average is 38%.[5]

I know that we've all seen this kind of data before, and it's easy to let
our eyes glaze over. But take a moment to let these numbers sink in. The
difference between the two schools is staggering. At the end of the 2018–
19 school year, not a single eighth grader from Manierre was proficient in
reading, compared to 81% of Lincoln eighth graders. These two schools
serve the same neighborhood and are a mere 1.3 miles away from each other.

And this is the twenty-first century, not the nineteenth.

I don't know why the kids from Manierre can't read. That would
require a deep look inside the school. Some of those kids appear to be
extremely impoverished and may come from troubled families. And one
can imagine that the teachers, no matter how skilled and how caring, have
a very difficult task. Concentrating all of the most troubled students in one
school building would not seem to be the best strategy for helping those
children. But, absent severe disabilities, any child is capable of learning to
read proficiently by the end of eighth grade. The one thing I know for
sure? The children are not to blame.

How does one child from Old Town end up at Lincoln, while another ends up at Manierre? Is it merit? Say, a test? Is it chance? Like a lottery? What does the application process look like?

Well, the Chicago Public Schools has split the community into two groups based on whether you live north or south of North Avenue. If you live north, you go to Lincoln. If you live south, then you're assigned to Manierre.

If these were health clinics or restaurants, there's no chance that such stark differences in performance would persist in establishments within walking distance of one another. If the families living south of North Avenue were allowed equal access to Lincoln, certainly some of them would apply to enroll their children there. For who can deny that a child will be better off at a school where 81% of the graduating students can read at grade level versus a school where none can?

But the children south of North Avenue aren't even allowed to apply to Lincoln.

Randall Blakey is the executive pastor of the diverse LaSalle Street Church just a few blocks south of Manierre. "If the Manierre parents had the same choices as every other parent north of North Avenue," he says, "I'm sure they'd take advantage of the choices."

"We fell in love with a townhome in Old Town," says Angela Mota, the parent of a four-year-old who will enroll in elementary school next year. She and her husband found out too late that their home is on the wrong side of the line. "We had to sell our old place as quickly as possible. We didn't do our due diligence."

"I thought Old Town had good schools," Angela remembers. "And then we got here, and it's like 'Oh, crap.'" It's clear that Manierre won't prepare their daughter to be successful in high school and beyond. The Motas still don't know what they're going to do, but they are determined to find another option. They are looking into magnet schools and other selective schools that have a very competitive application process in Chicago.

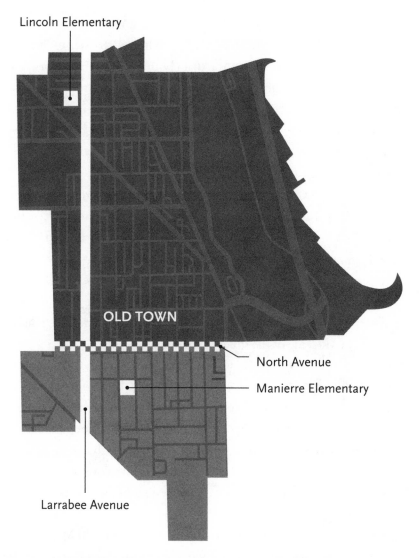

Figure 2.1 North Avenue is the boundary between the attendance zones of Lincoln Elementary and Manierre Elementary Schools in the Chicago Public Schools.

Source: Chicago Public Schools

Lincoln Elementary, a public school little more than a mile from their house, isn't an option. "I don't think Lincoln takes anybody off the wait-list," says Angela. "They have a huge population."

Brian Speck lives just a few blocks north of the Motas and is the father of two boys who have attended Lincoln. "There's a barrier to entry to Lincoln Elementary," he says, "And that's both good and bad." Brian says that he and his wife had their eye on one home that was south of North Avenue. "We really liked it, and it was $250,000 cheaper than the house we ended up buying," he remembers. "But private school in Chicago can run up to $40,000 a year." So they paid the extra $250,000 so that their kids could attend a "free" public school.

Even though Old Town residents cross back and forth over North Avenue every day, the school district does not allow them to traverse that magical boundary when they walk their child to school. District officials begin sorting and separating the local children when they are just five years old, as families start enrolling their children in public-school kindergarten. At this early age, the Manierre kids are trapped in failure. For a child growing up in Old Town, everything depends on whether you live on one side of the street or the other.

Is Lincoln Elementary a Public School?

There's a theory that says all of this is necessary. We need public schools, and it's important that families have access to neighborhood schools. So school districts draw school boundaries to make sure that each child can go to the school nearest her home. And the district adjusts the school boundaries over time based on where the kids are and which schools have extra room.

Under this theory, the differences between Lincoln and Manierre are merely accidental. One neighborhood school turned out better than the other. That's just the breaks. Or maybe it just so happened that the smarter kids all lived north of North Avenue. What could the school district do about that?

But I don't think that's what's going on here. I think there's quite a bit of evidence to suggest that wealthier residents of Chicago, working with elected politicians and top school officials, have used the school boundaries to capture Lincoln Elementary—nominally a public school—for their private benefit.

Let's zip back in time to 2013.

In 2013, the schools in the neighborhood were at a tipping point. Lincoln was 129% overcrowded,[6] partially due to young families moving into the school boundaries in order to gain access to the elite public school. Informed families assigned to Manierre, black or white, would seek out private schools or find another public option, such as a charter or a magnet school. This left Manierre less than half full, with lots of empty classrooms. Indeed, the district as a whole was facing an underutilization crisis and was planning on closing many schools.

The logical solution in Old Town would have been to redraw the attendance boundaries so that some of the Lincoln families would have been redirected to Manierre. Many Lincoln families in Old Town actually live closer to Manierre. If those families have a "neighborhood school," that school is Manierre, not Lincoln. Such a plan also would have been consistent with state law, which requires districts in Illinois to periodically redraw attendance zones for the "prevention of segregation and the elimination of separation of children in public schools because of color, race or nationality."[7]

But that's not what happened. Instead, top district officials proposed to close Manierre down and invest $19 million in a renovation of Lincoln that would increase the school's capacity. Would the additional space allow any of Manierre's children to transfer to Lincoln and finally escape their failing school? No, the addition would simply allow Lincoln to serve students in the existing attendance zone, but more comfortably.

Manierre's students would have been reassigned to Jenner Elementary, another failing school with excess capacity. A huge political fight followed. The Chicago Teachers Union filed a lawsuit to block the closure.[8] The lawsuit was dismissed, but eventually Manierre was allowed to stay open, partially because the Manierre students would have had to cross gang lines in order to get to Jenner, possibly putting them in physical danger.[9]

Meanwhile, Mayor Rahm Emanuel had no problem pushing through the unnecessary $19 million renovation of Lincoln Elementary in order to avoid sending some kids across North Avenue to fill the empty seats at Manierre. One insider told me, off the record, that politically power-ful parents in the attendance zone went to Illinois Senate President John Cullerton, who cut a deal with Mayor Emanuel and sent state funds to the Chicago Public Schools in order to ensure that the zone lines would not be redrawn.

Now Lincoln has a larger, updated building that is at 94% capacity.[10] According to the facilities data published by the Chicago Public Schools, the newly renovated building at Lincoln has a capacity of 1,080 students, but only 956 were enrolled as of the twentieth day of school in 2018. That meant there were 124 open seats at the school. Yet Lincoln still refuses to admit any students who live south of North Avenue.

Brian Speck, the Lincoln parent, was surprised at how it all went down. "The city is broke. The state is broke," he says. "And suddenly $20 million lands in your lap."

In a deposition in 2013, the chief administrative officer of Chicago Public Schools, Tim Cawley, insisted that families in Old Town couldn't be reassigned to Manierre "because it is highly disruptive to relocate people from their existing school to another school."[11] But he expressed no such concern about asking Manierre children to cross gang lines to attend Jenner.

The same lawsuit produced internal district documents in which offi-cials imagined that, once Manierre was shut down, its building could be "leveraged" to create a second campus for Lincoln. For that to work, Manierre would have to be "emptied" of the existing Manierre students.[12]

As noted in Chapter One, the original idea of a "public school" is that it's a place where everyone in a community can send their kids, a place where all the races and classes mix, and a place where less privileged kids have the same chances as anyone else. But that's not what Lincoln Elementary is.

You can't talk about Lincoln and Manierre without talking about race and income. Lincoln is 63% white, and only 14% of the students are low income.[13] Manierre's kids are 96% black and 4% Hispanic—and 93% low income.[14] Many Manierre kids come from the Marshall Field Garden Apartments, a subsidized housing development just south of North Avenue. Pastor Blakey says that many of the Manierre families are experiencing extreme poverty. As a result, schools like Manierre have been "under-resourced and under-enrolled."

Politically, Old Town leans left, like most of Chicago. I'll bet that the vast majority of Lincoln parents consider themselves liberal and abhor racism. Is there a chance that some of them have unconscious, or even overt, racial biases that would lead them to be reluctant to see their kids share a school with the kids from Manierre? Could be.

But race is not the core issue here. Race is not what's keeping kids out of Lincoln Elementary. What keeps Old Town kids out of Lincoln Elementary is geography—the artificial boundary of North Avenue.

There are lots of white families living south of North Avenue. The 60610 zip code, covering that portion of Old Town south of North Avenue, is 72% white. We can assume, based on the heavily black demographics of Manierre Elementary, that those white families are figuring out other options for their children. Indeed, the neighborhood's black alderman Walter Burnett told the *Chicago Tribune* back in 2013 that middle-class *black* residents of Old Town will not send their kids to Manierre.[15]

"If you're a middle-class parent in the Manierre zone," confirms Pastor Blakey, "you end up paying for private education, or you work your political connections to get your kid into a Selective Enrollment school."

Lincoln Elementary, though nominally public, appears to have been captured by a small group of private citizens and powerful officials who use attendance-zone boundaries to keep out most Chicago children. These politically powerful citizens are not the wealthiest of the wealthy, not the 1%. These are upper-middle-class families who are willing to pay extra to live within that section of Old Town that is assigned to Lincoln. During the controversy over Manierre's potential closure and Lincoln's renovation, one Lincoln parent admitted that those north of North Avenue feared that their property values "would plummet should the attendance boundaries be redrawn."[16]

Of course, these parents are just doing what they think is best for their kids—both the Lincoln parents who buy into the zone and the Manierre parents who look to escape a failing school. They're all working within the system that exists now, and we shouldn't shame them for that. We should applaud them for their willingness to do what is necessary for their kids to get a good education. Certainly if I lived in Old Town, there is no way that I would send my children to Manierre. No child should go to a school in which none of the graduating eighth graders show proficiency in reading.

Those Lincoln parents didn't get together and illegally conspire to take over Lincoln Elementary for privileged kids, keeping out families who could have benefited from access to the Lincoln education. Those parents probably didn't cut a corrupt backroom deal with Mayor Emanuel. But we all need to acknowledge that the school district has policies in place that allowed, and even encouraged, the school to be captured. Chicago Public Schools divides the Old Town neighborhood into two groups—those north of North and those south of North. Lincoln Elementary is empowered to discriminate against one group when they decide who is allowed to enroll. Savvy parents—rightly—do not want to be on the wrong side of that discrimination.

If only this were a problem unique to Chicago!

There are at least two other examples of urban school districts paying $12 million or more to renovate a school facility to add more seats, even though there was a public school just down the road with plenty of room. In Atlanta, residents of the Inman Park neighborhood convinced the school board to spend $18 million to build additional capacity at Mary Lin Elementary, so that the district wouldn't reassign their kids to another public school that had plenty of open seats and was within walking distance of Inman Park.[17] In Dallas, Lakewood Elementary got a $12.6 million renovation for the same reason.[18]

In each case, the school district caved to pressure from wealthy parents, who opposed changes to the school boundaries that would have reassigned their children from a high-performing school to a struggling school. Presumably, they also didn't want their property values to go down.

There are always eager parents, like those at Lincoln, willing to overpay for a house to get their child access to a high-performing, free public school. There are always bureaucrats who justify drawing their lines on maps in pursuit of the higher goal of "neighborhood schools," but who cave to political pressure in the end and draw the lines in a way that pleases wealthier parents. And there are always opportunistic politicians like Rahm Emanuel who will come to the rescue of an overcrowded school like Lincoln because it gives him an important education success story for speeches and elections.

It's a pattern that plays out every year in thousands of American neighborhoods.

Los Angeles—The Schoolhouse on the Mount

My family's neighborhood in Los Angeles is not so different from Old Town in Chicago. Like Old Town, the Mount Washington neighborhood is just a couple of miles from downtown and has seen a dramatic influx of young families since the Great Recession of 2008. Like Old Town, the neighborhood has seen many new restaurants and other small businesses open up to serve these families.

And, like Old Town, Mount Washington is home to one of the best public elementary schools in the city. Mount Washington Elementary sits atop a hill overlooking the more urban areas of Northeast Los Angeles. Here's how the school describes itself:

> Our students consistently score among the top schools
> in Los Angeles on the Academic Performance Index.
> Mt Washington Elementary School's dedicated teach-
> ers strive to enable all students to reach the standards
> by tailoring their instruction to individual student
> needs. Our instructional approach emphasizes prob-
> lem solving and learning by doing with an emphasis
> on the arts. In addition to a strong academic curric-
> ulum, Mt. Washington Elementary School features a
> comprehensive arts program and encourages students
> to participate in various activities designed to foster an
> appreciation of music, dance, and song. [19]

As it happens, for several years, the kids got to learn "music, dance, and song" from Louise Post, former frontwoman for indie rock band Veruca Salt. She was a Mount Washington parent who volunteered her time at the school.

Among the anxious parents of Northeast Los Angeles, one of the most popular topics is how to get your child into Mount Washington Elementary. And no wonder. Some of the surrounding schools are just not very good. Compare Mount Washington to Aragon Avenue Elementary, which is just over a mile away.

At Mount Washington, 75% of students meet the proficiency standard for reading on the California state tests. At Aragon Avenue, it's just 16%. The state average is 51%. [20]

Again, just as in Chicago, these two schools serve the same neighbor-hood and are just over a mile apart. How does the school district decide who goes where? The dividing line in this case is an utterly random, meandering mile-long attendance-zone boundary that wends through the neighborhood along Avenue 37, Roseview Avenue, and Cliff Drive, cutting across streets such as Killarney Avenue and Randall Court, sepa-rating neighbor from neighbor.

Figure 2.2 The attendance zones of Mount Washington Elementary and Aragon Avenue Elementary Schools in the Los Angeles Unified School District share an attendance-zone boundary that snakes through the Northeast Los Angeles neighborhood.

Source: Los Angeles Unified School District

As we've seen before, the artificial geographical boundary helps keep the two schools divided along race and class lines. Mount Washington is 59% white, and only 12% of students are low income.[21] Aragon is 95% Hispanic, and 88% of students are low income.[22] In fact, Mount Washington is surrounded by zones for seven other traditional public schools. Only one of those schools has a population of white children of more than 5%—Aldama Elementary, which has 9% white students.

But the attendance zone knows no color! There are many white children who actually live closer to Mount Washington Elementary, but they live outside the zone boundaries and are therefore excluded. Mount Washington is an island of privilege in a working-class ocean.

My own kids and many of our neighbors' kids, of all ethnicities, are in this category. We are excluded from Mount Washington Elementary, even though it is the closest school to our house. The district map assigns our family to Glassell Park Elementary, which is struggling in much the same way that Aragon Avenue is.

For our family, at least, this isn't a huge concern. We have the resources to send our kids to private school, if necessary, and we also have the savvy to navigate the Los Angeles Unified School District's byzantine system of school choice. Although we feel the injustice acutely, and it may cost us tens of thousands of dollars in private school tuition, it is likely that we will be able to find a school that is a good fit for our kids and that performs better than their assigned school.

For families with lesser means, this geographical exclusion is a much bigger issue, one with life-altering consequences.

Los Angeles is a little bit different from Chicago in one key way. In some years, a handful of families from outside the attendance zone are allowed to enroll in Mount Washington. One way around the boundary is to apply to a special gifted-and-talented program, and the other is to apply for a "permit" for out-of-boundary admission. I'll talk about the problematic nature of gifted-and-talented programs in Chapter Six. For now, let's just say that access to such programs is not always fair and equitable.

As for the "permit" process, it requires you to get "released" from your assigned neighborhood school, and it only works if there is space at the school you've selected. You read that right: One school has the right to deny you permission to go to another school. The official policy of LA Unified is that requests cannot be denied "based solely on reduction of student population at the school of residence."[23] Because the schools are budgeted on headcount, each lost student means lost revenue, giving the schools a powerful incentive to reject transfers.

Nevertheless, the district lists a finite number of approved reasons why a family should be granted a release, so the burden of proof is on the parent. There are lots of stories of parents arguing and pleading with the principal of a struggling school, who is reluctant to see one more child go. It's as if you needed permission from your current doctor, who has a successful treatment rate of 15%, to switch to another doctor who has a success rate of 75%.

The fact remains that a geographic boundary, drawn by school-district officials, prevents the vast majority of area families from gaining access to the best public school in their neighborhood. Los Angeles parents are hyperaware that similar lines keep middle-class and working-class children out of other elite public elementary schools in the city, from Ivanhoe in Silver Lake to Canfield on the Westside, from Carpenter in Studio City to Wonderland in Laurel Canyon.

Philadelphia—The Penn Alexander Miracle

These same themes play out, in a slightly different way, in the University City district of Philadelphia. In 2001, the School District of Philadelphia opened up an innovative new school in partnership with the University of Pennsylvania and the Philadelphia Federation of Teachers. Unlike many new public schools, this school would be a "neighborhood school," serving the local blue-collar population, which was majority African American. The attendance zone would be carved from the existing attendance zones of surrounding schools.

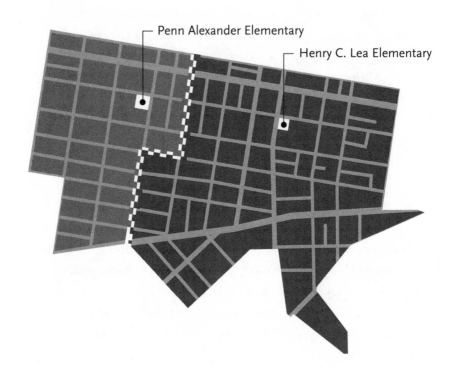

Penn Alexander Elementary

Henry C. Lea Elementary

Figure 2.3 In Philadelphia, the attendance zones of Penn Alexander and Henry C. Lea Elementary Schools share a boundary of two-thirds of a mile along 46th and 47th Streets.

Source: School District of Philadelphia

The school has become an astounding success story. In this past year, 86% of Penn Alexander students were proficient in reading on the Pennsylvania State Assessments, and 77% were proficient in math. Children at a neighboring school, Henry C. Lea Elementary, showed the opposite pattern of performance: 33% proficient in reading and only 15% in math.

The two schools share an attendance-zone boundary for about two-thirds of a mile, running along 46th and 47th Streets. Kids on the unlucky side of that line are not even eligible to apply to Penn Alexander.

The twist in Philadelphia is that it's not just those outside the attendance zone who are excluded. Because of Penn Alexander's reputation, young families have been moving into the "catchment area" (Philadelphia's name for an attendance zone). Many families have paid a $100,000 premium (or more) for a home in the catchment area. But the school is now full, and many of those families' kids will not be able to attend Penn Alexander.

A study by the Penn Institute for Urban Research found that home prices in University City rose by 175% in the thirteen years after the new school was announced. Within the Penn Alexander catchment area, the increase was almost twice as high—320%.[24]

By creating a geographical enrollment preference for this elite school, the School District of Philadelphia inadvertently and bizarrely created the conditions for thousands of low-income residents to be displaced. Take a step back and consider what happened here. Philadelphia fixed a troubled school, finally giving hope to poor families who had long lived in the neighborhood. Then the middle-class hordes came swooping in, pushing home prices (and rents) up and pushing the longtime residents out of the neighborhood and out of the school. Any family who moved to a more affordable area would no longer be allowed to enroll their kids in the school.

It's tragic.

Twenty years ago, nobody foresaw what was about to slam University City—drastic gentrification spawned by something as simple as opening a school that was able to help kids to achieve at their grade level. One landlord evicted all low-income tenants in 2018, then listed the property for sale for over $2 million, justifying the price by noting that the building falls "within the limited, highly sought-after Penn Alexander School Catchment."[25] Never mind that the catchment area is now so packed that living within it is no longer a guarantee of admission.

With low-income families forced out of the catchment area, the demographics of the school have changed dramatically. A school that was conceived for and intended to help an underserved majority African American population now serves a population that is 40% white and 22% Asian. African American children now make up just 20% of the student body.[26]

Meanwhile, the parents who moved into the catchment area became outraged when they realized they had overpaid for their house or apartment and now might not be able to send their kids to their chosen school:

> [We] moved to ensure that our kids would get into what was then the best school around....The school also CONSISTENTLY assured us that we were guaranteed spots b/c of where we lived. And now they want to pull this crap.[27]

> What about enforcing the current catchment rules? The best guess is that 20–30% of students at the school do not live in the catchment.[28]

> Great ideas here! We should round up all of the PAS students in little rows in the schoolyard and demand to see their papers! Those who [are] unable to prove residency will be stripped of their PAS sweatshirts, banned from the school and forced to walk home to whatever stupid neighborhoods they actually live in. This is totally the best and most productive direction

for everyone's energies! Way to go![29]

It seems pretty clear that the housing boom in the catchment area was driven by this school and that neither [Penn Alexander] or the district are responsible for this and have zero obligation to do anything more than they already are. Welcome to the neighborhood and good luck![30]

I for one need to start saving money… for not only did we pay a lot for our house… but in a few years we may also need money for private school. I feel we did not get what we paid for… [31]

Not everyone in the catchment is well off. There are poor families living here, we sacrifice a great deal to afford these overpriced apartments just so our kids can get a good education.[32]

A Nationwide Pattern

Chicago, Los Angeles, Philadelphia—Unfortunately, this pattern is not confined to just three American cities. It repeats itself over and over from the Northeast to the Deep South, from California to the Pacific Northwest, from Texas to the Upper Midwest. Always the same: Two neighboring schools share an attendance-zone boundary, which separates the neighborhood kids into two groups. And the two schools look completely different in terms of student performance and demographics.

This is an American phenomenon.

Appendix A documents fifteen more such cases, showing just how widespread the pattern is. And these are just a few examples. Look for your city on the list:

Atlanta
Mary Lin Elementary vs. Hope-Hill Elementary (p. 186)

Columbus
Clinton Elementary vs. Como Elementary (p. 188)

Dallas
Lakewood Elementary vs. Mount Auburn Elementary (p. 190)

Denver
Cory Elementary vs. Ellis Elementary (p. 192)

Fort Lauderdale
Bayview Elementary vs. Bennett Elementary (p. 194)

Indianapolis
Center for Inquiry 84 vs. Butler University Lab School 55 (p. 196)

Jacksonville
Hendricks Avenue Elementary vs. Spring Park Elementary (p. 198)

Los Angeles (Silver Lake)
Ivanhoe Elementary vs. Atwater Ave. Elementary (p. 200)

Los Angeles (Westside)
Canfield Ave Elementary vs. Crescent Heights Blvd Elementary (p. 202)

New York (Brooklyn)
PS 8 Robert Fulton vs. PS 307 Daniel Hale Williams (p. 204)

New York (Upper West Side)
PS 199 Jessie Isador Straus vs. Riverside School (p. 206)

Oakland
Peralta Elementary vs. Sankofa Academy (p. 208)

San Diego
Chesterton Elementary vs. Linda Vista Elementary (p. 210)

San Jose
James F. Smith Elementary. vs. John J. Montgomery Elementary (p. 212)

Seattle
John Hay Elementary vs. Lowell Elementary (p. 214)

A Phone Call to Lincoln Elementary in Chicago
A staff member answers the phone, "Lincoln School."

Hi, my name is Tim. I'm a prospective parent. My wife and I are moving to Chicago in a couple months, and we're looking into school options for our kids.... We've heard really great things about Lincoln. I don't understand exactly how it works in Chicago. If we get a place south of North Avenue outside the attendance zone, is there a way to apply to the school to get in? How does that work?

"No, no. It is a neighborhood school. It's an attendance area... The school where your address is, that's the school you would go to. So if you want your child to go here, you have to move within the boundaries."

It does look like the houses north of North Avenue are more expensive, obviously.

"North of North Avenue? Yeah. Where are you coming from?"

We're moving from the West Coast.

"Oh, okay. This is definitely a neighborhood school."

And the school is full? In LA, there are special programs you can apply for to get into the school. Is there anything like that?

"They do have that, but it's only if we should, like, lose some students. And it doesn't look like it. That's where that waitlist comes in."

I assume you've been full because you're such a good school.

"Exactly, exactly."

So if we buy into the attendance zone or rent within the attendance zone, are we automatically into the school?

"Yes, you're automatically in. You just have to show proof."

Chapter 3
Educational Redlining

———————————

Note this moment at the end of the last chapter: The staff member at Lincoln Elementary asks for "proof" of your address before you can enroll your child at the school. This is a moment that happens thousands of times every year in America. This is precisely the moment I want to examine in this book.

How strange it is!

- Imagine you show up at a nearby emergency room with a broken arm, and the nurse at the front desk asks for proof of your address before taking you in for an X-ray.

- Imagine you walk into the neighborhood branch of your city's library. You sit down at a computer, and a librarian comes over to check your ID. "Sorry," she says. "I know you live in the city, but you're assigned to a library two miles away. You'll have to leave."

- Imagine that there's a fire in the neighborhood, and the Station 22 fire truck won't water down your home because the truck's onboard computer shows that you're just over the line, zoned for Station 44.

The staff member at Lincoln Elementary isn't simply trying to ensure that you live within the jurisdictional boundaries of the Chicago Public Schools. That would make some sense, because you might not want nonresidents coming in and getting a free education at schools that were paid for by resident taxpayers.

No, this employee at Lincoln Elementary is interested in whether you live on the right side of an *attendance-zone boundary*, which is a line drawn around the school by the district staff. The key question is: What empowers the staff at the school to ask for proof? What empowers them to turn away students who don't live in the attendance zone?

The short answer is—state law.

This is the great secret of public education in the US. In many states, there are little-known state laws that require or allow school staff to ask this question and make enrollment determinations based on where a family lives within the district. In other states, there are simply no laws that prevent school officials from drawing attendance-zone boundaries. It is implicitly allowed.

This is how two schools like Lincoln and Manierre, so close in proximity, can remain so separate. State law and district policy work together to prevent the families who attend failing Manierre from simply crossing North Avenue and enrolling their child at thriving Lincoln.

What is this peculiar, misshapen thing that we call an "attendance zone"? It's a license to discriminate. If the school is full (most of the best schools are), then the attendance zone provides the school with legal cover to exclude families who live within the district's jurisdictional boundaries but outside of the arbitrary zone for that school as drawn by district bureaucrats.

In a stroke of Kafkaesque perversity, the official policy of the Chicago Public Schools, empowered by Illinois state law, instructs the office manager at Lincoln Elementary to use the child's address to determine whether or not she can enter through the schoolhouse door.

Recently I called up the office at coveted John Hay Elementary in the hilly and affluent Queen Anne neighborhood of Seattle. This is a school that bears a strong resemblance to Lincoln Elementary in Chicago. To enroll your kids at John Hay, a staff member tells me, "You want to be on the north side of Denny Way." Otherwise your kids will be zoned to go to struggling Lowell Elementary, and the district is "pretty strict" about the zones. "It is unfair," she says, "but you have to have boundaries somewhere. Otherwise no one would want to go to that school [Lowell]."

I take her point about the lack of parent demand for failing schools like Lowell. But actually she's wrong about the need for attendance zones. There are other ways for schools to decide who gets in. Public charter schools, for example, hold open lotteries when applications exceed the number of open seats. In most states, charter schools are *forbidden* from discriminating against families based on where they live within the school district. The open-to-all policy for charters is the result of political battles led by teachers' unions and school boards to prevent charters from cherry-picking the students they enroll.

Indeed, there are several states, my home state of California being one, in which traditional public schools are *required* to discriminate based on residential address, and public charter schools are explicitly forbidden from doing exactly that. See Appendix B for a full list of states where the public schools operate under these paradoxical requirements.

Many traditional public schools have no need to discriminate when they enroll children for the school year. They operate below their full capacity and have lots of empty seats, and every extra student is welcome, bringing with them additional per-pupil funding from the state and/or the federal government. In Los Angeles and other cities, district enroll-ment has fallen significantly in recent years due to declining birth rates and the increasing popularity of charter schools. So the vast majority of schools, ranging from abysmally bad to mediocre, have space and will welcome new students from outside the attendance zone.

But, even in Los Angeles, the elite public schools are a different story. They have no empty seats. They're full because demand exceeds supply. As we saw in the previous chapter, young families will crowd into an attendance zone, just to gain access to an elite school. I'm defining *elite* here based not on any objective criteria but simply on the excess demand for that school and the resulting difficulty of getting a child enrolled. Typically, these elite schools have higher test scores, more experienced teachers, more enrichment programs, more engaged parents, and a more rigorous curriculum. They also have lower levels of absenteeism, discipline issues, and incidents of violence. Because the school is full, the staff at a public school like Lincoln have no choice but to discriminate in their enrollment decisions. They can't admit everyone who wants to go there.

We already have a name for this practice of using your address to determine whether or not you are eligible for valuable government services. We call it *redlining.* The name comes from government maps created during the New Deal. These maps used the color red to indicate those urban neighborhoods that were "hazardous," which mostly meant that those areas were majority black or Hispanic. People in these red-shaded portions of the map were ineligible to qualify for some federally subsidized mortgages. In guidelines published by the Federal Housing Administration, the federal agency warned lenders to avoid neighborhoods with schools "attended in large numbers by inharmonious racial groups."[1]

These racially biased policies had a huge impact on who did and didn't qualify for mortgage loans during the New Deal era, and that in turn has influenced the fate of those neighborhoods almost a century later. The *Washington Post* journalist Tracy Jan writes, "Racial discrimination in mortgage lending in the 1930s shaped the demographic and wealth patterns of American communities today."[2]

In this chapter, I want to explore how state laws create the conditions for separate-and-unequal schools within a single neighborhood. Although every state is different, some common themes emerge. I want to draw a direct line from the racially discriminatory housing practices of the middle decades of the twentieth century and the laws and policies that create attendance zones for public schools today. Redlining in the housing market was outlawed back in the 1960s and 1970s, but educational redlining is still with us. They don't call it redlining, though. Sometimes they call it "open enrollment."

California and the Myth of Open Enrollment

California is an instructive example of how educational redlining can be institutionalized in the law.

Like most states, California delegates to local school officials the implementation of its constitutional promise of public education. Over time, the state legislature has become more and more active in regulating the public schools and their operations. For decades, nowhere in the state's voluminous Education Code did the state legislature explicitly empower local school districts to create attendance zones.

That all changed in 1993. In that year, both Republicans and Democrats were looking for ways to open up more school choices for California families. There was a consensus that many public schools, especially in poorer urban areas, had been failing persistently for decades. One potential solution was to allow students to transfer to other public schools, so the legislature passed a wave of laws promoting public school choice.

In late 1993, Republican governor Pete Wilson signed into law Assembly Bill 1114, which required California school districts to offer "open enrollment" to students who live within the district, meaning that any student could apply to any school in the district, not just their assigned school. The bill was written and sponsored by Democrat Dede Alpert from Rancho Santa Fe.

The open enrollment law was pitched as a way to increase choice without supporting school vouchers. "This was an opportunity to show that it's not choice we object to, it's the tax-financed vouchers for private schools we object to," Alpert said back in 1993 after the passage of the bill.[3]

The Open Enrollment Act of 1993 requires school districts to establish an open enrollment policy "as a condition for receipt of school apportionments from the state school fund."[4] For most districts, that makes it mandatory, as they can't survive without their state funding allocation. Resident parents, then, are free to "select the schools [their] child shall attend, irrespective of his or her residence in the district." So far, so good. The year after it passed, the *New York Times* wrote that California's Open

Enrollment Act was "the most sweeping choice plan in the country, affecting 5.7 million children."[5]

It was, however, a false promise. A key clause in the law requires that "no pupil who currently resides in the attendance area of a school shall be displaced by pupils transferring from outside the attendance area."[6] With that one sentence, the law allows—even requires—that districts continue to discriminate based on residential address. It also guarantees that most California kids will continue to be locked out of the elite public schools. Because those elite public schools are already full, any new transferring student would, by definition, be displacing someone already living within the attendance area.

The irony is this: In California it is the "open enrollment" law that is keeping the doors of the elite public schools closed to most children. And this type of law is common across the country. Of the states that require districts to offer open enrollment within the district boundaries, at least ten include an explicit exception for schools that are already full with families who live in the school's zone. In all of these states, elite public schools are legally protected from having to admit students from outside the zone.

Twenty-five years after its passage, the effect of California's law is clear when you look at the Los Angeles Unified School District (LA Unified). What LA Unified calls its "open enrollment policy" is primarily concerned—paradoxically—with the ways in which the school district can deny you fair access to a school that you'd like your child to attend.

The district publishes a document called "Guidelines for Enrollment Transfers," which outlines what students can and cannot do. The very first point, A1, simply paraphrases the state law that allows elite public schools to lock out most kids: "No kindergarten–12th grade student who currently resides in the attendance area of a regular school shall be displaced from that school by open enrollment transferred students."[7]

What's more, the program is discretionary, giving tremendous power to school administrators. The school principal determines whether or not to offer any available slots to children from the general public. Even if the school is not operating at capacity, the district gives very clear instructions to principals that there is no legal obligation to open up the school's enrollment: "It is not mandatory that any school take part in the Open Enrollment program."[8] Note that it is not consistent with the law for the district to give a principal this discretion of publicizing open seats or not, because the Open Enrollment law requires that any resident parent be given the choice of the school their child will attend, if there is space available.

Two elite public schools in Los Angeles—Mount Washington Elementary, featured in Chapter Two, and Ivanhoe Elementary, profiled in Appendix A—chose not to make any spots available to children via the Open Enrollment program in 2018–19.[9] In fact, I've been unable to find evidence that these schools have ever offered Open Enrollment spaces to students living outside their attendance zones. The truth is that the officials at these schools have a very clearly defined constituency: the families who live within the borders of the attendance zone, many of whom bought their houses precisely to be a part of that constituency. Los Angeles families who live outside the zone *have no claim* on these public-school officials.

I analyzed LA Unified's Open Enrollment list for 2018–2019 in order to understand where the open seats are. What I found shouldn't surprise you—The best schools have almost no open spots. In a district with over four hundred elementary schools, there are only sixteen schools in which 80% of the fifth graders demonstrate reading proficiency. Of those sixteen schools, only one offered any open seats. That one school, Roscomare Road Elementary in pricey Bel Air, lists only two available spots. That's *two classroom seats* available at high-performing schools—in a district serving more than 275,000 elementary students.

But there are almost 3,000 seats available in lower-quality schools.

Those two open seats at Roscomare represent just 0.02% of the total enrollment at the sixteen high-performing schools. At all the other

elementary schools in LA Unified, open seats are 1.2% of the total enrollment. That's more than a 60x difference.

This analysis of LA Unified likely understates the disparity in available
classroom seats by quite a bit. Tanya Anton, a public-school admissions
consultant whom we'll meet in Chapter Six, says that there's "no way"
that the Open Enrollment list "reflects the ACTUAL number of open
seats across LA Unified, only the numbers the district 'announces.'"[10]

Anton says there would be a "public outcry" if the district announced
the true number of open seats, because it would reveal that the district
has been lying to charter schools about the lack of free space, which
the district is required to offer to charter schools when it is available. In
addition, the public would likely balk at providing billions of dollars in
additional funding for facilities if they knew that so many of the schools
are operating at much less than their physical capacity.

Anton points to one school that the district lists as "full." At Mark Twain
Middle School on the west side of Los Angeles, the district reported zero
Open Enrollment spots available in fall 2018. Back in 2003, before student
losses began to hit LA Unified hard and district officials were pitching
the public on billions of dollars in bonds to fund the construction of new
schools, Mark Twain enrolled almost 1,400 students. Now enrollment has
collapsed to 731.[11] But according to the district's Master Planning and
Demographics Unit, those seats just disappeared, and Mark Twain is now
so full that it can no longer accept Open Enrollment students.

Schools like Ivanhoe and Mount Washington are clearly operating at or
near their true physical capacity. So, what about those unreported open
seats in empty classrooms? They are clustered in underperforming schools.
Mark Twain ranks below the state average in reading and math proficiency,
and we can surmise that Mark Twain would have close to 1,400 students
enrolled if it performed like Ivanhoe or Mount Washington.

This isn't just a problem in Los Angeles. In cities across the US,
high-performing public schools like Ivanhoe Elementary and Mount
Washington Elementary are not really open to the public.

Different State Laws, Same Results

Across the fifty states, there is tremendous variation in how state laws regulate the assignment of students to public schools. The ultimate result, however, is remarkably consistent across the states: Attendance zones are used to grant preferential enrollment to elite public schools that operate at full capacity due to excess demand from parents.

And, despite the existence of a variety of programs that allow families to select a school that is not their assigned neighborhood school, attendance zones remain tremendously important in the allocation of educational resources and opportunities. In 2016, 78% of US public-school students attended their zoned school.[12] For families who live within the zones for these elite schools, it is likely much higher, probably over 90%.

In most states, local authorities are given a vast amount of discretion in determining which students go to which schools. In Ohio, for example, the legislature provides that "the superintendent shall assign the pupils to the proper schools and grades."[13] This empowers districts to create attendance zones, but does not require it.

In nearby Pennsylvania, state law explicitly requires that every school district carve itself up into attendance zones:

> The board of school directors of every school district
> or joint school shall, for the purpose of designating
> the schools to be attended by the several pupils in the
> district or area served by the joint board, subdivide
> the district or joint school in such manner that all the
> pupils in the district shall be assigned to, and reason-
> ably accommodated in, one of the public schools in
> the district or joint school.[14]

Note that California and Pennsylvania take very different approaches—on the surface. In a law passed in the 1940s, Pennsylvania explicitly requires school districts to grant geographic enrollment preferences. California has no explicit requirement, but it tucks an implicit requirement into its

1993 "open enrollment" law, which forbids a student from outside the attendance zone from displacing one from inside the zone. In each case, state law requires the district to set up the zones and discriminate against children who live outside the zone, if the school is full.

For many states, I've been unable to find any statutes that specifically address student assignment or the creation of attendance zones. In these states, the long-standing principle of local control dictates that school districts are free to establish attendance zones, as well as the geographic enrollment preferences that come with the zones.

Appendix B profiles twenty-five states where attendance zones may be vulnerable to legal challenge, including an overview of statutes and constitutional provisions relevant to student assignment, attendance zones, and the provision of public education. More on this in Part III.

Educational Redlining in 21st-Century America

As discussed earlier, redlining is the practice of denying services to the residents of particular neighborhoods. The most well-known examples involved home mortgages or banking services, which were denied to heavily African American neighborhoods for much of the twentieth century. The US has a well-documented history of discrimination in the real estate market perpetrated by both private companies and government agencies.

The term *redlining* itself gets its name from the Home Owners' Loan Corporation (HOLC), a federal agency that provided mortgage relief to borrowers who were under threat of foreclosure. The HOLC created maps showing that certain neighborhoods—predominantly black neighborhoods—were high risk and therefore ineligible for federal assistance. These neighborhoods were highlighted in red as "hazardous."

In his 2017 book *The Color of Law*, Richard Rothstein of the NAACP Legal Defense Fund details how the federal government used progressive housing programs to maintain a "state-sponsored system of segregation."[15] President Roosevelt's New Deal programs were used to deny service to black neighborhoods and keep other neighborhoods all white. State and local policies, as well as the practices of private banks, had similar effects.

"Private prejudice, real estate steering, bank redlining, and income differences all certainly played a role," Rothstein told Terry Gross on the NPR program *Fresh Air*. "But without federal policy designed explicitly to segregate every metropolitan area in this country, those private factors would not have been able to successfully segregate their communities."[16]

Educational redlining is analogous to redlining in the housing market. In each case, valuable government services are reserved for more privileged communities, using geographic preferences as a way to limit who is eligible to receive them.

Both sets of policies emerge from a similar political dynamic:

1. Politicians of both parties preach the value of government-provided services, creating government programs that distribute billions of dollars in aid.

2. Public agencies draw lines on maps showing who gets what.

3. Many middle-class and lower-income families find themselves ineligible because of where they live.

4. Politicians defend the discrimination on the basis of practical considerations, such as protecting neighborhood integrity.

Redlining in real estate was made illegal by Congress with the passage of the Fair Housing Act in 1968 and the Community Reinvestment Act of 1977. Public agencies and private businesses are now forbidden from using these tactics that reinforced racial divisions and inequality.

But it's absolutely certain that, even today, attendance zones are contributing to the ongoing division of our country along the lines of race and class. Wealthier families cram into the attendance zones of desirable schools, and poorer families are boxed out. Because income and wealth disparities correlate with racial differences, this inevitably leads to more racial separation as well.

Educational redlining not only echoes the ugly history of discriminatory housing policy and redlining in the mortgage market but also builds off of that past discrimination. Many neighborhoods show patterns of economic and racial divisions that directly align with redlining maps from the 1930s or the placement of federally sponsored housing developments that were designated for one race or the other.

A 2016 study by the National Community Reinvestment Coalition (NCRC) found that 74% of neighborhoods marked red for being "hazardous" back in the 1930s remain low-to-moderate income today, while areas marked as "best" in the 1930s are still 91% middle-to-upper income. And nearly two-thirds of the "hazardous" areas still have greater than 50% minority population, while 85% of the "best" areas are still predominantly white.[17]

"It's as if some of these places have been trapped in the past, locking neighborhoods into concentrated poverty," Jason Richardson, director of research at the NCRC, told the *Washington Post* when the study was released.[18]

By carving up our cities into attendance zones, we are perpetuating the economic and racial divisions that marked one of the darkest eras of our nation's past. Indeed, in some neighborhoods, you can still see the ghost of the redlining map when you look at a current map of the local school's attendance zone.

Figure 3.1 shows the current Ivanhoe attendance zone[19] superimposed on the HOLC redlining map of the Silver Lake neighborhood of Los Angeles from 1939. Like Mount Washington Elementary, Ivanhoe Elementary is one of the elite public schools in Los Angeles that is protected by an attendance zone. Note how the minority neighborhoods of Silver Lake remain on the outside looking in.

Eighty years after the creation of the map, the schools that serve the red and yellow areas of the map are still all majority Hispanic, while Ivanhoe is 75% white.[20]

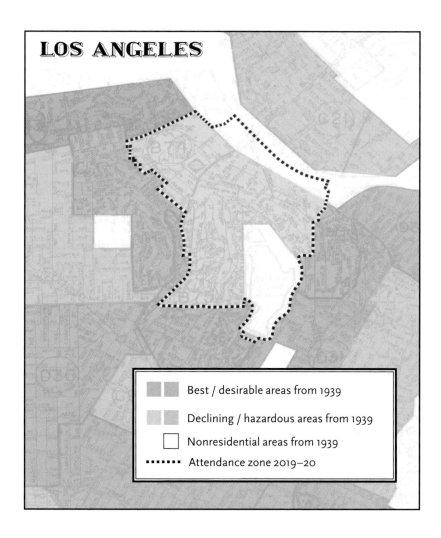

Figure 3.1 The attendance zone for coveted Ivanhoe Elementary School in Los Angeles excludes minority neighborhoods labeled "hazardous" or "declining" on the government's redlining map from 1939.

Source: Los Angeles Unified School District, US Home Owners' Loan Corporation

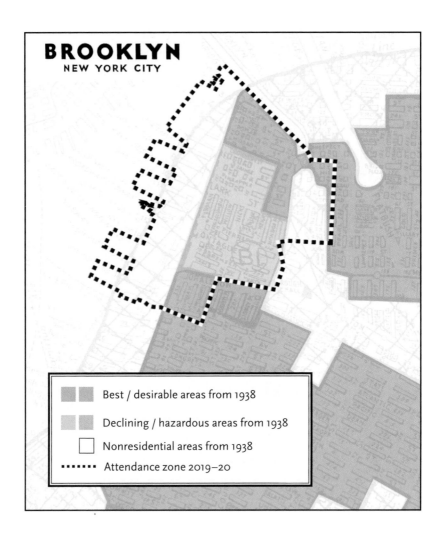

Figure 3.2 The attendance zone for elite elementary school PS 8 Robert Fulton in Brooklyn excludes minority neighborhoods labeled "hazardous" on the government's redlining map from 1938.

Source: New York City DOE District #13, US Home Owner's Loan Corporation

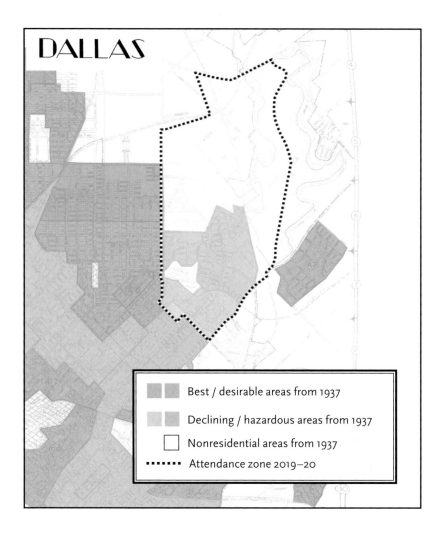

Figure 3.3 The attendance zone for Lakewood Elementary in Dallas covers land that was undeveloped in 1937, but the southern portion of the zone boundary replicates exactly the border between "desirable" and "undesirable" areas from the government's redlining map.

Source: Dallas Independent School District, US Home Owners' Loan Corporation

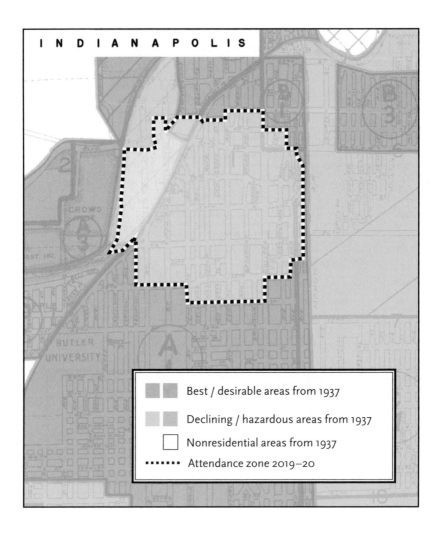

Figure 3.4 The attendance zone for one of Indianapolis's most exclusive public elementary schools—Center for Inquiry 84—excludes minority neighborhoods labeled "hazardous" or "declining" on the government's redlining map from 1937.

Source: Indianapolis Public Schools, US Home Owners' Loan Corporation

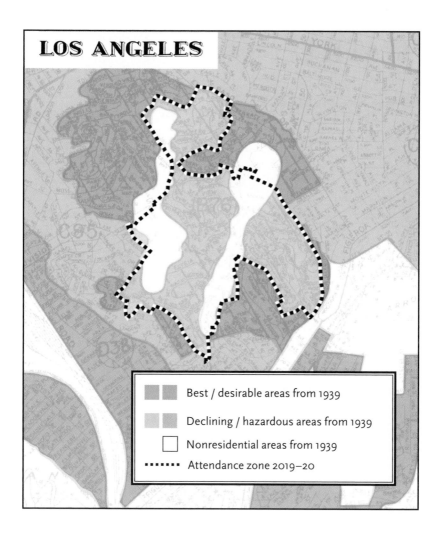

Figure 3.5 The attendance zone for coveted Mount Washington Elementary School in Los Angeles excludes minority neighborhoods labeled "hazardous" or "declining" on the government's redlining map from 1939.

Source: Los Angeles Unified School District, US Home Owners' Loan Corporation

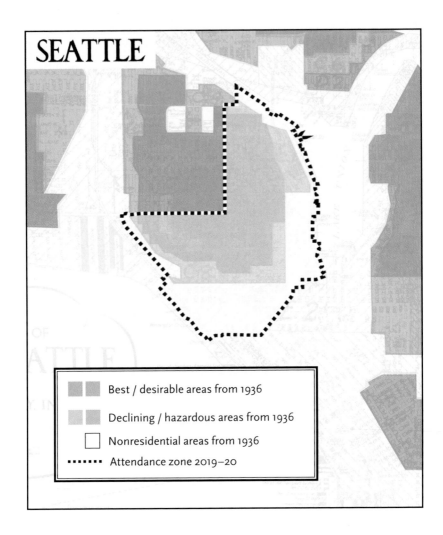

Figure 3.6 The attendance zone for high-performing Hay Elementary in Seattle largely covers a section of the city labeled as "desirable" on the government's redlining map from 1936.

Source: Seattle Public Schools, US Home Owners' Loan Corporation

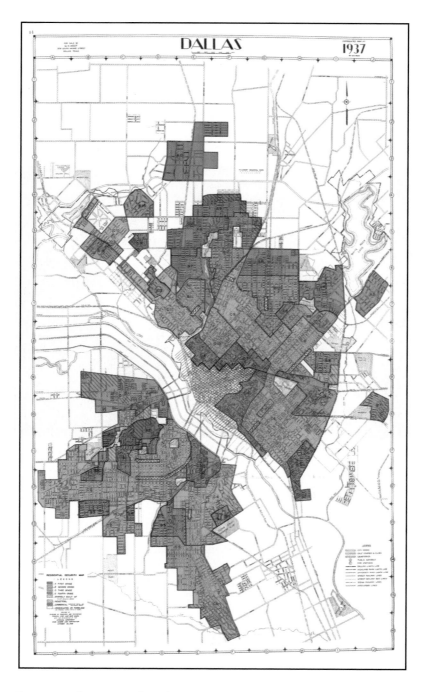

Figure 3.7 Redlining maps from the New Deal era were used by a federal government housing agency to mark minority neighborhoods as "hazardous" or "declining" and therefore ineligible for mortgages and/or housing assistance.

Source: US Home Owners' Loan Corporation

Figures 3.2–3.6 show similar maps for other attendance zones in Brooklyn, Dallas, Indianapolis, Los Angeles, and Seattle. In each case, to varying degrees, today's geographic discrimination still reflects the patterns of racial and geographic discrimination of the mid-1900s. Figure 3.7 depicts the full 1937 redlining map for Dallas, showing that a federal government agency deemed a majority of the city's neighborhoods to be "hazardous" or "declining."

In some cities, the geographic discrimination has evolved over time. In Chicago, for example, the "desirable" areas on the North Side have changed, so the attendance zone of Lincoln Elementary no longer reflects the divisions of eighty years ago. But somehow, neighborhoods with significant minority populations still find themselves on the wrong side of the line.

Scientists who study attendance zones acknowledge that the existence of these zones is the primary cause of the persistent racial divisions in our public schools. One team funded by the National Science Foundation found that dramatic differences in the racial composition of public schools are now "driven primarily by residential segregation. Compact attendance zones replicate the racial composition of local areas. As most local environments are racially homogeneous, so are school attendance zones."[21]

Meredith Richards, a professor at Southern Methodist University, conducted a quantitative analysis of attendance zones in Massachusetts and found that the zones led to a greater degree of racial separation than would have emerged had students simply been assigned to the public school closest to their home:

> The gerrymandering of educational boundaries
> generally fosters inequities in access to educational
> opportunities and worsens already severe levels of

racial segregation in schools... The historical record
abounds with examples of attendance zones being
gerrymandered in a racially discriminatory fashion.[22]

    Given that the stakes are so high, it's no wonder that attendance-zone
boundaries are politically contentious and subject to political shenanigans.

    Imagine the machinations that went into drawing the torturous outlines
of the attendance zone in Birmingham, Alabama, shown below.[23] From
the map, we can't tell why it was drawn like that.

    In 1967, the historian Meyer Weinberg wrote a fascinating book called
Race & Place: A Legal History of the Neighborhood School. Weinberg showed
that, in many districts, the school boards created attendance zones in the
1950s and 1960s to replace the former system of school assignment by race.
And they gerrymandered the boundaries so as to keep the races separate,
while avoiding the explicit racial segregation that had been forbidden by

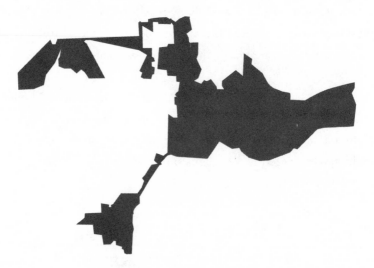

Figure 3.8 Attendance zones in Birmingham, Alabama, are extremely irregular in
shape and do not reflect natural geographic boundaries or neighborhood identities.
Source: Birmingham City Schools

the courts. This happened in Hempstead, New York, for example.[24] The districts used geography as a proxy for race.

In rarer cases, the boundaries were gerrymandered to break down the previous patterns of segregation. But no matter the goal, an attendance zone always creates sharp inequalities of opportunity for families who live in the same neighborhood. Some children will be allowed to enroll in the best public schools, and their playmates across the street will be excluded because of where they live.

A growing number of education leaders have recognized that school assignment based on residential address is perpetuating both racial divisions and stark inequalities of educational opportunity. Richard Kahlenberg, a senior fellow at the left-leaning Century Foundation, told *ReasonTV* in 2016 that public schools with true open enrollment "offer the possibility of higher levels of integration" than do schools defined by geographic attendance zones.[25]

And, in a recent opinion piece in *The Hill*, African American parents' rights advocate Virginia Walden Ford argues that a system of truly open schools is the "fastest track to integration" because it "uncouples the decisions about where to live and where to send children to school."[26]

Of course, attendance zones are only one of two types of geographic enrollment preferences. In the next chapter, I'll turn to the separate but related issue of the lines *between* school districts (rather than the lines drawn *within* a single district). These district boundaries, too, have a long history of being used to create separate and unequal schools.

Chapter 4
The Jurisdictional Affliction

"We bought our house because of the schools," says Jennifer DeRoche of Milwaukee, Wisconsin. "But they weren't the right fit for our kids."[1]

After getting married and having their first daughter, Jennifer and her husband, Tom (my cousin), started thinking about where their kids would be educated. The DeRoches are in the dead center of the middle class: Tom runs training programs for a nonprofit, and Jennifer works part-time as an academic counselor at the University of Wisconsin-Milwaukee.

Tom and Jennifer knew they wouldn't be able to afford the elite private schools on the north side of Milwaukee. So they started researching public-school districts.

Like many young middle-class families in Milwaukee, they eventually decided they were willing to pay a significant premium to buy a house within the boundaries of the heralded Whitefish Bay Schools. "We moved to Whitefish Bay because we thought it had the best schools," says Jennifer.

Twenty years later, she wishes they hadn't done it. "If I knew then what I know now," she says, "we never would have moved to Whitefish Bay."

By the time their older daughter, Natalie, was ready to enroll in high school, they had already decided that they needed to find another option. "Natalie came home from her first day of eighth grade and said, 'I don't want to go to Whitefish Bay High School,'" Jennifer recalls. "The competitive nature of the schools in Whitefish Bay is really unhealthy. Most of those girls suffered from anxiety and depression. They were all medicated."

The problem, says Jennifer, is that a middle-class family who can't afford private schools is in a very difficult position. They have to pick a school when they buy their house, which is often years before the children start kindergarten. "When you have a two-year-old, you have no idea. The school that is the 'best' is the school that is best for your child. And there's no way to know that until years after you paid for the house." They ended up enrolling Natalie in a performing arts charter school in Kettle Moraine, over forty miles from their home in Whitefish Bay.

Two years later, they were struggling to find a school for their younger daughter, Meghan, who had very specific needs that didn't seem to match any available school environment. First they tried Whitefish Bay, and the district would not approve of additional services that Meghan needed. Then they tried the charter school that her sister attended. That didn't work either.

They finally settled on Shorewood High School, a public high school just down the road from their house, even closer than the high school in Whitefish Bay. But, because of where they bought their house fifteen years before, they found themselves on the wrong side of the district boundary.

So they rented an apartment in Shorewood and used that address to get Meghan admitted to Shorewood High. It was a way of "gaming the system," says Tom. "It was very hard on Meghan, because she wanted to immerse herself in her new school. But she couldn't invite her friends over to the house."

Yes, it's a complicated game, and parents of all income levels are at the mercy of arcane district rules. For the Shorewood schools, the residency requirements were strict. "In Whitefish Bay," says Jennifer, "we only had to verify our address to enroll in kindergarten. But in Shorewood you've got to show two different pieces of proof every year you enroll."

So, after a year, when it became clear that Meghan was thriving at Shorewood High, Tom and Jennifer sold their house in Whitefish Bay, the home where they'd raised Natalie and Meghan since they were toddlers. They bought a new house less than a mile away in Shorewood. Suddenly they were legal again. "We couldn't just buy a new house that first year," says Tom, "because we didn't know if the school was going to work for Meghan."

That said, they still hadn't wanted to sell their home in Whitefish Bay, which was filled with so many emotional memories. "We never would have moved," says Jennifer, if school access hadn't been an issue. "It was stressful for everybody. But I don't regret it."

She can see, though, that not every family has the time or resources to find the right school for their children. "Thank God I was only working part-time," says Jennifer. "The amount of time and energy I've put into this over the last ten years is incredible. If you're a low-income person working two jobs—even if you have the desire—you don't have the time and the resources to figure it out. The system doesn't work in an easy way."

District Boundaries

There's a key legal distinction between the two types of educational boundaries. Attendance zones are *administrative service areas*. Government employees carve up the map and determine who gets preferred enrollment at what school. There are no elected officials at the attendance-zone level, and the residents of an attendance zone are not subject to special taxes.

School-district boundaries, by contrast, are *political subdivisions*. They are jurisdictional. As governmental entities, school districts are typically overseen by elected or appointed school board members. School districts often have the legal authority to assess taxes on their constituents or issue bonds in order to fund the district's activities.

In nine states, including many in the South, the schools are operated directly by city or county governments and are just a "department" of a larger organization. In states where the school districts operate independently of local municipalities—such as California, Illinois, and Texas—the districts operate as "special-purpose governmental entities" that often cut across city and county boundaries. Other states, such as New York, have a mixed setup in which most schools are operated by independent school districts, but others are operated by city governments. In New York, the five largest cities, including New York City, all operate the local schools directly.

Like attendance zones, school-district boundaries dictate which schools a child is allowed to attend. But there are differences in how the two types of boundaries play out. School districts usually encompass a much larger area, so families who seek to move to a specific district are often making a decision to move much farther away, rather than just a few blocks. This would affect, for example, a family with young children moving out of the city center and out to a suburb with higher-performing schools.

Picking a District

When Tom and Jennifer DeRoche bought their house in Whitefish Bay, they were utilizing the most common form of school choice—moving to a district that is perceived to have better schools. In many areas of the country, where districts are tightly packed, school-district boundaries become extremely important for young families deciding where to live.

For the DeRoches, moving into the city of Milwaukee would not have been a great option. Even the most sought-after schools in the Milwaukee Public Schools are rated as mediocre. Golda Meir School, Fernwood Montessori, and Maryland Avenue Montessori are considered the best public schools in Milwaukee, and none has more than 56% of its students proficient in reading or 46% proficient in math.[2] Although the state standards differ between Wisconsin and Illinois, notice the dramatic difference compared to one school in central Chicago, Lincoln Elementary, where 85% are proficient in reading and math.[3]

Schools in the suburbs of Milwaukee have much better student achievement. Whitefish Bay, which is one-twentieth the size of Milwaukee, has two elementary schools where over 65% of students are proficient in each subject area, well above the state average.[4]

	TYPE OF EDUCATIONAL BOUNDARY	
HOW THEY DIFFER	**School District**	**Attendance Zone**
How big?	Larger, often covering dozens or even hundreds of square miles.	Smaller, often covering just a few square blocks or a neighborhood
Who creates the boundaries?	The state legislature (established by state law)	District officials (drawn by district staff)
How do you change the boundaries?	Politically, by an act of the legislature or a vote of the people	Administratively, decided by district employees
How can you escape?	Cross-district (or "inter-district") open enrollment created by state law and/or district-to-district agreements	Within-district (or "intra-district") open enrollment created by magnet schools, charter schools, and other district programs
What's the punishment for using someone else's address?	Often includes payment of back "tuition" for the "stolen" educational services, plus jail time	Usually no punishment, except that the child is removed from the school and sent back to the assigned school
Are there per-pupil funding disparities?	Yes. Districts usually get less funding if local property taxes are lower. In some states like California and New Jersey, the state is the primary funder of public schools, which typically reduces cross-district spending discrepancies. More about this in Chapter Eight.	Yes. Schools get more or less funding depending on school-board policies that decide the winners and losers in resource allocation, including policies that (1) assign more experienced teachers to schools in wealthier areas, (2) establish special programs at some schools and not others, and (3) direct special federal or state aid to schools that serve students with a higher level of need.

Table 4.1 Unlike attendance-zone boundaries, school-district borders carry the weight of the law.

Like attendance zones, school-district boundaries exacerbate the economic and racial divisions in our public schools. In many cities, it is very common for wealthier families to move to the suburbs in order to take advantage of higher-performing schools. These suburbs—and their schools—are much more homogeneous than the typical neighborhood in the city center.

In these wealthier suburban districts, property tax revenue is significantly higher because suburban real estate is often much more expensive. These suburban districts, then, often have significantly more funding per pupil. In many states, this funding discrepancy has led to civil rights lawsuits aiming to equalize funding across districts. Although some have been successful—notably in California, Kentucky, and New Jersey—the vast majority of these lawsuits have failed to mitigate significant cross-district spending differences. More about this in Chapter Eight.

Genevieve Siegel-Hawley, a researcher who has devoted her career to studying educational boundaries, believes that this dynamic is the primary reason for the ongoing racial divisions in our schools: "The majority— between 60 and 70 percent, according to some estimates—of school segregation can be attributed to how students of different races are sorted across district boundaries."[5]

Two Blocks Away from the Country Club of Detroit

Look, for example, at Mack Avenue on the east side of Detroit. For a stretch of over a mile, students on the northwestern side of Mack Avenue are assigned to Marquette Elementary–Middle School. Less than 5% of Marquette students are proficient in reading or math, at any grade level. Marquette's student population is over 91% low income and 99% African American.

Now step across the street. On the other side of Mack Avenue, you're no longer within the borders of the Detroit Public Schools. Now you're in a different district—the Grosse Pointe Public Schools. And your five-year-old is zoned to go to one of three schools: Lewis Maire Elementary,

Richard Elementary, or Kerby Elementary. Lewis Maire is the most diverse of the three, and it serves only 4% low-income students.

A child living just southeast of the intersection of Mack Avenue and Moross Road is literally living less than two blocks from the country club. The prestigious golf and social club the Country Club of Detroit is right at the corner of Moross and Chalfonte Avenue. That child could walk to three schools where proficiency rates in reading and math are over 80%. But she isn't allowed to enroll in these schools.

Instead the child is assigned by law to go to a school that is 91% low income, with proficiency rates lower than 5%. Whatever educational programs are in place at Marquette Elementary, they aren't working for those kids.

Like many states, Michigan has a law allowing for "interdistrict" or cross-district open enrollment. In theory, a family should be able to walk across Mack Avenue and enroll their child in one of the high-performing schools in the Grosse Pointe district.

But that's not how it works. Michigan law *allows for* cross-district enrollment, but it doesn't require it. Grosse Pointe is closing two elementary schools due to enrollment decline over the last several years,[6] and the district is considering additional school closures.[7] But the district still refuses to admit students from the other side of Mack Avenue or anywhere else outside its boundaries. Indeed, while the district struggles with declining enrollment, it requires parents to submit four documents proving residency before it will enroll a child.[8] The kids just across the street aren't welcome.

To keep those families out, the district maintains an anonymous tip line for the public to report enrollment by nonresidents, and the district typically investigates between one hundred and four hundred students per year.[9] It's a twist that echoes the work of the famous Stasi agency of East Germany, which employed citizen informants to tattle on their friends and neighbors in order to crack down on anyone opposed to the repressive communist government.

But Michigan isn't unusual in limiting cross-district enrollment. In addition to allowing districts to opt out, other states make it difficult for families to access schools in other districts by (1) allowing districts to charge "tuition" to out-of-district families,[10] (2) providing exceptions for districts whose schools are at capacity, or (3) requiring families to get approval for the transfer from their home district.[11]

In California, the amount of cross-district enrollment has increased dramatically since 2009, when the state legislature eliminated the requirement that parents be "released" by their home district.[12] Prior to 2009, districts had been reluctant to approve out-transfers, as it meant a corresponding loss of per-pupil funding from the state.

Now you don't need approval from your home district, but you still need to be welcomed by another district in the state. Becoming a "District of Choice" (one open to transfers from external families) is still up to that district's board, however, and only 43 of 977 districts (less than 5%) participated in the program in 2018–2019.[13] So cross-district open enrollment is very frequently a false promise, much like the within-district open enrollment policies outlined in Chapter Three.

(I'll also note here that a District of Choice is forbidden from discriminating against out-of-district students based on where they live and must instead hold a "random drawing" if it receives more applications than the number of seats it has reserved for open enrollment.[14])

In Ohio, one foundation has taken an aggressive approach to overcoming enrollment restrictions associated with school-district boundaries: They're moving one hundred inner-city families from poor-performing districts into high-performing districts that refuse to accept open enrollment kids who live outside the district borders.

In Columbus, the Move to PROSPER project is providing subsidized housing to one hundred low-income families, helping them move from struggling urban school districts into higher-performing suburban districts.[15] The targeted suburban communities—Dublin, Hilliard, Gahanna, Olentangy, and Westerville—have all refused to participate in cross-district open enrollment.[16] But they won't be able to exclude the Move to PROSPER families once those families have established legal residence, something that would have been impossible without philanthropic subsidies.

The fault lines of American democracy often trace the winding boundaries of school districts.

Secession and Gerrymandering

Given what's at stake—enrollment preferences at high-performing schools—it shouldn't be surprising that school-district boundaries can get caught up in political shenanigans.

The nonprofit EdBuild has documented forty-seven cases since 1986, including thirty-six since 2000, in which a new district has been created by seceding from a larger district.[17] In the vast majority of cases, "the communities involved were less diverse and had higher property values than those they left behind."[18]

One judge in Alabama approved the secession of the city of Gardendale from the Jefferson County school system, despite finding that "race was a motivating factor" in the secession effort. Gardendale is 78% white, while the rest of Jefferson County is 55% nonwhite and has a poverty rate nearly three times that of Gardendale.[19]

What's more, there is empirical evidence that existing school-district boundaries contribute to greater levels of racial and economic isolation. One study looked at four states that have similar demographics, all with nonwhite populations within the narrow range of 46%–50%. Two of these states, New York and New Jersey, are highly fragmented by small school districts. By contrast, North Carolina and Virginia are much less fragmented, more like Figure 4.1 on the following page.[20]

In the highly fragmented states like New York and New Jersey, the schools are much more strongly divided along racial lines.[21]

Ironically it is the northern states, not the southern states, that typically see higher levels of school-district fragmentation and the resulting

Figure 4.1 School-district boundaries are much more fragmented in New York and northern New Jersey than they are in southern Florida. *Source: Bischoff, based on data from the National Center for Education Statistics (2007).*

STATE	Fragmentation of school districts	Number of "intensely segregated" schools (90-100% nonwhite)
New York	High	1 in 3
New Jersey	High	1 in 5
North Carolina	Low	1 in 10
Virginia	Low	1 in 20

Table 4.2 States with a high level of fragmentation of school districts experience more racial division than do states with low levels of fragmentation. *Source: Ayscue and Orfield.*

divisions along racial lines at the district level. Many southern states have county-wide school districts, which leads to an overall district population that is much more diverse and representative of the entire community. Of course, in those southern states, attendance zones still restrict enrollment at the elite public schools within those districts, and those elite public schools are typically much less diverse than the district as a whole.

Policy analyst Jon Shure traces the intractable problems of racial divisions in the New Jersey schools directly to the fragmentation of school districts:

> It's the reality that while [New Jersey] is one of the
> nation's most diverse states, it's also where minority
> public students are less likely than in almost any other
> state to go to a well-integrated school—a conse-
> quence of having so many small, homogeneous
> districts.[22]

Kendra Bischoff, a sociologist, has found that metropolitan areas with more fragmented school districts not only have more racially isolated schools but also more racially isolated neighborhoods.[23] That could be because white families, with higher levels of wealth on average, use that wealth to buy premium houses in the desirable districts, leading to even more racial separation over time.

"A Kind of Monopoly on Education"

One state legislator in Atlanta has decided to confront this issue head-on. Rep. Valencia Stovall represents Ellenwood, Georgia, a predominantly African American city not far from the city center of Atlanta. In 2018, Stovall proposed HB788, which would make "address borrowing" fully legal and effectively eliminate school-district boundaries (and attendance boundaries) for many students:

> A student shall be allowed to attend and be enrolled
> in the school for which a parent or guardian certifies
> that an individual residing in the school's attendance
> zone has authorized such parent or guardian to use
> such individual's address for purposes of establishing
> residency.[24]

Stovall learned about a case in Ohio in which a low-income parent was convicted and imprisoned for using her father's address to get her kids into a better suburban district. Stovall wanted to find out if the same kind of thing was going on in Georgia. She sent data requests to several high-performing suburban districts and found that, yes, many of them were investigating parents and kicking children out of schools for using false addresses.

"People in the better neighborhoods get a better education," says Stovall. "Better teachers, more resources." She says that geographic enrollment restrictions have a negative impact on school quality. "Everybody in the district knows that you can't go anywhere else, so they don't have to pay attention to quality. They have a kind of monopoly on education."[25]

Stovall's colleagues have thus far refused to bring the bill up for a vote in the Georgia legislature.

PART II: PEOPLE DO ANYTHING TO GET THEIR KID IN

Chapter 5
Don't Fence Me In

"We all used that address," says Heather Yang. "Me and all fifteen of my cousins."[1]

Heather (not her real name) is the daughter of Chinese immigrants and grew up in the San Francisco Bay Area. "My family was on the wrong end of the Cultural Revolution," she says, referencing Mao Zedong's effort in the 1960s and 1970s to "cleanse" Chinese society of capitalists and other Chinese citizens who opposed his communist ideology.

Her parents and many members of her extended family moved to the Bay Area. But the Yang family was not wealthy. Most of her family rented apartments or bought small, inexpensive houses in East Oakland, across the Bay Bridge from San Francisco. "We came here for a better opportunity," Yang says.

Her mom and dad enrolled her in a neighborhood school in East Oakland. But it quickly became clear that it wasn't going to work for seven-year-old Heather. "As a first grader," Heather recalls, "I remember thinking, 'Ohmigosh, I'm bored.' I wasn't getting appropriate instruction for my grade level. My parents decided it was not going to fly."

With her cousins all experiencing similar frustration with other Oakland schools, the family decided to take action.

"My mom and her siblings were able to afford one house in Alameda," says Heather. "They had to pool their resources to do it." Alameda, a suburb of Oakland bordering the San Francisco Bay, has a school system, the Alameda Unified School District, that is known for the academic rigor of its public schools.

So all sixteen of the Yang family cousins used that one address to gain access to the Alameda schools. "There were times it was an hour-and-a-half car ride to school," Heather says, recalling the daily commute from East Oakland. "You had to cross bridges and train tracks."

"Our house was in a predominantly white catchment area," she says. "I think the school knew that it was suspicious. They would swing by the house. The office manager at the school was not kind to my parents. We heard about people getting kicked out of the schools, but it never happened to us."

As the family began to work their way out of poverty, several of Heather's aunts and uncles were able to afford apartments within the boundary lines of the Alameda Unified School District. "We swapped addresses with other families within Alameda," she says. "Just to get access to the better schools."

It worked for the Yang family. "Every single one of my cousins went to college," says Heather proudly. Her older cousins started at local community colleges, but the family got better at leveraging their educational opportunities over time. Heather herself, one of the younger cousins, graduated from Stanford a few years ago and now works in nonprofit devoted to improving the educational choices available to low-income families.

"The educational opportunities paid off for us," says Heather. "My parents really value education."

She draws a direct line between discriminatory housing practices of the mid-twentieth century and the current policies that restrict students' educational choices based on where they live. "Redlining was very strong in Oakland," Heather says, and minorities clustered in the neighborhoods in the "flatlands" of Oakland where they were legally allowed to reside. Now the residents of these neighborhoods, still primarily minorities and immigrants, are assigned to neighborhood schools that are generally failing.

Heather points out that there are higher-quality schools in the Oakland

Hills, but those schools are closed to anyone who lives down the hill. "Even now, if you live in the flatlands," she says, "some families only have a choice between a school that sucks and a school that sucks more."

It's not just the schools that suck. The whole system sucks. We've taken this incredibly precious resource—a quality education for our children—and restricted access to it based on where you live. That's *obviously* bad for a low-income family who lives on the "wrong" side of town and can't afford to move to the "right" side.

But is it good for anyone? Is there anyone benefiting in the long run?

Suppose that your family is a bit wealthier, and you want to keep your kids in the public schools. Our current system asks you to select a home based on the school you think will be best for your children. You're often buying a house five to ten years before your kids enter school. What if the neighborhood school takes a turn for the worse in the intervening years? What if the school turns out to be a poor fit for your child? What if you get a job offer that you can't refuse on the other side of town? Or—heaven forbid—what if the attendance zone changes, and your house drops in value by $200,000 overnight?

Or imagine that you are a middle-class couple without kids, and you don't intend to have them. You may find that you're priced out of your favorite neighborhood because all the young families are willing to pay a premium for access to the school, which you will never use.

How coercive these policies are! They separate us from each other, sorting American children into the "haves" and the "have-nots" before they even enroll in kindergarten. These policies push up home prices in many attractive neighborhoods, limiting housing choices for millions of American families. They force us to pay hundreds of thousands of dollars for access to schools that are supposed to be open to the public. Or they force us to navigate a byzantine bureaucracy in order to help our children escape from a failing neighborhood school that they have been assigned to. For those of us who don't have the wealth to buy a new house or the free time to navigate the bureaucracy, they force us to make agonizing decisions that will affect the fate of our children for decades to come.

How we contort our behavior to make these policies work for us! They motivate many of us to lie about where we live. They push some parents to "rat out" their children's playmates for using a false address. They turn educators into spies, forcing them to conduct Stasi-style home checks and then kicking kids out of school because they don't live on the right side of the street. They put some of us in jail for trying to get the best education for our kids.

Ask your friends. Ask your neighbors. Ask yourself.

How have these policies affected you and the people you love?

"We Had to Be Very Specific with Addresses"

When investment banker Sundus Kubba and her husband, Joe Kazemi, a statistician, moved to New York City from the Midwest, they intentionally sought out the attendance zone of PS 87, a very desirable school on the Upper West Side.

"We had to be very specific with addresses," Kazemi told the *New York Times*, even paying attention to "what side of a street an apartment was on."[2]

While they had no intention of living on the Upper West Side for the long term (it is much too expensive), they were aware that the New York Department of Education has a policy that is widely known as "Once you're in, you're in."

It means that the department only checks your family's residency when a student enrolls. If the family later moves, the student is allowed to stay enrolled at the former neighborhood school. According to school-district officials, this is for the good of the kids. "When students jump from school to school ...," spokesman Devon Puglia told the *Times*, "personalization is difficult."

For Kubba and Kazemi, the policy allowed them to get their daughter into a high-performing school; over 80% of PS 87 students are proficient in reading and math.[3] A year later, they bought a two-bedroom apartment in Hamilton Heights. "We can get more for our money uptown," said Kazemi, noting that a similar apartment on the Upper West Side would have cost the family at least $300,000 more. In Hamilton Heights, the family is zoned to attend PS 153, a school where proficiency rates are less than 40% in both reading and math.[4] Luckily, the couple's daughter, Maya, was already "in" at PS 87, and she wasn't forced to transfer to the struggling school.

According to one expert on public schools in New York City, many families will rent for even less time than did Kubba and Kazemi. It's "fairly common," this expert says, for families to sublet an apartment for just one month in order to get their child into a school that they will attend for up to nine years.

"I Realized We Weren't in the Zone"

Amanda and Daniel Turner (not their real names) moved to Los Angeles in their twenties to work in technical jobs in the entertainment industry. They had gotten married after graduating from Boston College in Massachusetts. In the wake of the real estate crash of 2008, they were able to buy a nice home in the Mount Washington neighborhood just north of downtown.

They didn't have kids yet, but they knew that Mount Washington Elementary was one of the highest-performing public elementary schools in all of Los Angeles. So they were set for the next twenty years of their lives.

A few years later, after having their son, Colby, Amanda started looking at schools. She was surprised to learn that they are *not* zoned for Mount Washington Elementary but are instead zoned to go to Glassell Park Elementary, a school with very poor student achievement just down the hill.

"I guess I was a little naïve to think that Mount Washington School covered all of Mount Washington," says Amanda now. "I didn't realize that the zones are different."[5]

In the years since Colby's birth, housing prices in Los Angeles have doubled, meaning it won't be possible for the family to move to a better school zone. "I don't know what we're going to do," says Amanda.

"So Many Families Are Moving into the Zones"

Lakisha Young is the executive director of Oakland REACH, a nonprofit that coaches low-income parents on how to get the best education for their child. "During open enrollment," says Young, "you can theoretically choose any school in Oakland. But we have an access problem."[6]

She notes that most of the best schools are located in the Oakland Hills, which are predominantly upper income and white. "There's such a small number of high-quality schools," she says. "People buy into those neighborhoods."

Peralta Elementary is one example of a higher-performing school that is in the flatlands of Oakland, which has historically been more working class. At Peralta, 82% of students are proficient in reading and 77% in math, and only 17% of students are low income.[7] At nearby neighboring Sankofa Academy, 8% of students are proficient in reading and 5% in math.[8] Over 82% of the students at Sankofa are low income, and 71% are African American. These two schools are just *three blocks away from each other.*

Given how much Peralta outperforms Sankofa and other neighboring schools, it should be no surprise that Peralta is over capacity, partially due to families trying to take advantage of the attendance zone. "So many families are moving into the zones with the good schools," laments Young, "it makes it harder and harder for others to get into those schools."

She reports that there have been efforts to merge the attendance areas of Peralta and Sankofa, as Sankofa has extra space. But the families at Peralta have resisted the move. "This is a very liberal city where people go on 'equity walks,'" says Young. "But when you ask them to push a chair over for a black kid coming in …"

She doesn't finish her sentence.

"The Rosa Parks Moment for Education"

Kelley Williams-Bolar wanted better schools for her kids. "I was worried about safety," she told the *New York Times*. She lived within the boundaries of the Akron Public Schools, about forty miles south of Cleveland. Williams-Bolar's father lived in the highly desirable Copley-Fairlawn City School District, which had lower levels of crime and higher student test scores. So Williams-Bolar used her dad's address to enroll her two daughters in Copley-Fairlawn.[9]

The district, however, caught on. They hired a private investigator to follow Williams-Bolar and document the fact that her children were living full-time in Akron. They kicked her daughters out of Copley-Fairlawn. Eighteen months later, the district prosecuted Williams-Bolar for fraud and larceny. Williams-Bolar spent nine days in jail before then governor John Kasich used his executive authority to reduce her sentence.

In her willingness to disobey laws in order to get the best education for her children, Williams-Bolar generated significant sympathy across the political spectrum. Commentator Kyle Olson told NPR that this was a "Rosa Parks moment for education and education reform."[10] An NPR caller noted that the Ohio courts have ruled that cross-district spending discrepancies violate the state constitution, but the state legislature has not done anything to change the funding mechanisms. "So I see it more as an act of civil disobedience," the caller said.[11]

For Williams-Bolar and her family, the whole incident was traumatic. "Both my daughters were devastated," she told the *New York Times*. "They still have moments where they think Mommy is going to be taken away."

Williams-Bolar isn't the only parent in jeopardy. Similar charges have been brought against other working-class or lower-income parents using someone else's address to get their children access to better schools. Hamlet Garcia faced up to seven years in jail for using his father's address to enroll his daughter in a high-performing school district in suburban Philadelphia. Garcia eventually pled guilty and had to pay restitution of $11,000 to the district.[12] Something similar happened to Yolanda Hill in

Rochester, New York[13]; Charles Lauron in Louisville, Kentucky[14]; and many others.

"Our Nanny Started Getting Mail at Our House"

Jeff Bedford and his wife, Susan (not their real names), live in the Silver Lake neighborhood of Los Angeles. Their nanny, Blanca, a native of Guatemala, lives about five miles away in Koreatown, but spends five to six days a week at the Bedfords' house. Blanca told Jeff and Susan that she was worried about the safety of her son at the local high school in Koreatown.

Later, she said that her son had been admitted to coveted Marshall High School, which is the neighborhood high school for Silver Lake. "How did that happen?" Jeff remembers his wife asking. "She told us, 'It's because of where I work.' We assumed she had gone through some process."[15]

Then they started getting mail addressed to Blanca at their home.

Right away they knew what had happened—Blanca had listed their address as her own. "If she would have asked," says Jeff, "we would have absolutely [allowed her to use our address]. She's so generous with our family. But we felt a bit hoodwinked."

"We Were Very Scared of Doing Anything Illegal"

"We had a very good life back home in Iran," says Manijeh Naficy. "But we gave all that up. All we wanted was for our kids to be happy and healthy."[16]

Manijeh's husband, Mo, had worked as an executive at a state-run television network in Iran in the 1970s. They were traveling in California when the Islamic Revolution erupted in Iran in 1979. They soon learned that Mo had been targeted for execution by the new regime, so they were unable to return home.

They settled into a working-class neighborhood in the San Fernando Valley, and the two of them got entry-level jobs at a small bank. They eventually had three children, and the family often borrowed addresses in order to get the kids into better public schools within the Los Angeles Unified School District.

Their youngest daughter, Shahrzad, was zoned to go to Reseda Senior High School, which had a reputation for drug use and low levels of academic performance in the 1990s. "I called a well-off friend who lived south of Van Nuys Boulevard," recalls Manijeh. "I asked if I could visit her, and I told her the situation. They gave us their utility bill, and they said it was okay to say that we were living with them."

With that utility bill, Shahrzad was able to attend higher-performing Birmingham High School. "We were very scared of doing anything illegal," says Manijeh now. "But we didn't have a choice. Our children's education was everything."

Thirty years later, Birmingham still outperforms Reseda. In 2018, 70% of Birmingham's students were proficient in reading, compared to just 47% of students at Reseda.[17]

Chapter 6
Consultants, Address Cops, and the
Price of a Public School

"We specialize in hidden gems," says Grace Lee Sawin, founder of Chicago School GPS. "You have your neighborhood school, but also a lot of other options… even if you can't afford to buy a house in Lincoln Park and send your kid to Lincoln Elementary."[1]

It's a commonly held belief in many American cities that you've got to pay extra for a house in order to get your kids into the "right" elementary school. But there will always be those families who can't afford to pay the premium or who fall in love with a home on the wrong side of the line. For savvy middle-class families in this predicament, a cottage industry has sprouted up to help their kids escape the schools they've been assigned to.

Chicago School GPS is one of a handful of small companies that support parents looking to find the right public school for their child. In Los Angeles, Tanya Anton started the GoMamaGuide to help parents navigate the student assignment policies of Los Angeles and other local districts. In New York, Robin Aronow started School Search NYC, and Joyce Szuflita started NYC School Help, which both provide similar services.

In the US, parents generally fall into one of three categories when it comes to how they select a school for their kids:

The Address Pickers. These parents pick a home at least partially based on the quality of the assigned public school. This includes both (1) families who move to the suburbs to access suburban districts with higher levels of student achievement, and (2) urban families who look very closely at attendance zones and may pick a house because it is on the "right" side of the street and is zoned to go to a higher-performing school in the urban center. These families are often paying a significant financial premium for their home, and they feel forced to decide where their children will go to school years before the kids enter the school. Another type of Address Picker is the lower-income immigrant family who puts five kids into one bedroom of an overpriced apartment within the zone of a high-quality school. According to the National Center for Education Statistics, 15% of American families select a home based on the assigned public school.[2]

The School Shoppers. These highly engaged families may not have the resources to buy their way into the best public schools. But they take advantage of state laws and school-district policies that give them some degree of control over what school their child attends. Many of these families may buy a home in a zone with an underperforming school, because it costs less money. They then look at a wide range of school options: charters, magnets, or gifted-and-talented programs. Typically, these parents devote significant time and energy into evaluating different options and filing the appropriate application paperwork. This category would also include families who make the choice to send their children to private schools or to homeschool them. These folks make up 31% of American families, including 19% who utilize public school choice and 12% who select private education options.[3]

The Obedient. Many families do not have the time, the money, or the inclination to actively select a school for their children. Some of these are upper-middle-class parents who just passively go along with the crowd and assume that their assigned suburban school is good enough. Other families may be struggling with job losses, illness, mental health issues, or anxiety about their legal status. Regardless of their circumstances, these are the families who reflexively enroll their children in the school assigned to them by the local district. This is often the neighborhood school. In the poorest urban neighborhoods, this is often a failing neighborhood school. The Obedient make up 54% of American families.[4]

Grace Lee Sawin and the other public-school admissions consultants primarily serve the School Shoppers (though they will, on occasion, also help the Address Pickers identify districts or zones to target when they are buying houses). For a family who can't afford the premium for a sought-after zone, spending $500 or so on a consultant gives them access to expertise on how to get their child into a high-performing magnet, a charter, or a gifted-and-talented program.

These consultants are in a unique position to see how district policies distort the behaviors of young families. Common behaviors emerge across all cities: (1) paying a housing premium for access to an elite public school, (2) utilizing special programs and selective schools to escape a neighborhood school that is underperforming, and (3) utilizing false addresses to access highly desirable schools (and hoping to avoid any audits or investigations conducted by school authorities).

In each city, the rules are a little bit different, so the parents' machinations have their own local flavor.

"What's Different About New York City"

Joyce Szuflita of NYC School Help told the *Atlantic* that many of the best elementary schools serve "a curated class of parents because they chose to move into the zone of the school they wanted."[5] These are the Address Pickers. When parents can't (or don't) pay the housing premium, they apply to "choice" schools or highly selective gifted-and-talented programs. These are the School Shoppers who seek out help from NYC School Help.

"The policies are very complicated," says the other New York consultant, Robin Aronow. "Even I'm confused, and I spend a lot of my time on this. What's different about New York City is that we also do a lot of [school boundary] rezoning. People can buy an apartment in an area zoned for one school, and by the time the child is old enough, they're no longer zoned to go there. You can go from the best school to the worst school overnight."[6]

Aronow tells of one nursery school director who allowed all her parents to use her address when applying to the neighborhood elementary school, which was at capacity. "The most popular schools end up with waitlists. Even if you live in the zone, you're not guaranteed a seat. You might get sent to the next closest school with space."

One anonymous school staffer told a blogger that the manipulation of waitlists by public-school employees is routine:

> No parents should trust a waitlist. I work in a public school. I help with registration. I can see how we move kids around. For example, if a parent knows the parent coordinator or someone in the school, they are moved to the top.[7]

As I discussed in Chapter Five, New York has a policy of "once you're in, you're in" for elementary schools. Savvy parents are known to rent an apartment for just one month, so that their kid will get into the desired kindergarten and be guaranteed access to that better school all the way through eighth grade.

"Your Kids Can Test Into Good Schools"

Grace Lee Sawin of Chicago School GPS spends much of her time helping middle-income parents find an escape route from a local neighborhood school that is underperforming. As in many other cities, the gifted-and-talented (G&T) programs often allow savvy parents to escape the attendance zone of an underperforming school. "Your kids can test in to good schools," says Sawin, meaning that the child's performance on a test will determine whether or not she can enroll at the school. "People are starting to realize that some of these Selective Enrollment schools are just as good as the schools in the suburbs."

But, again, upper-income families (often white or Asian) are much more likely to participate in G&T programs. Nationwide, almost 8%

of white students and over 13% of Asian students are enrolled in public G&T programs, while less than 5% of African Americans and Hispanics are in these programs.[8] Researchers have found that if you compare a black student and a white student at similar levels of achievement, the black student has only half the chance of being designated for a G&T program.[9] They show that, relative to black teachers, nonblack teachers are much less likely to identify a black student as qualified for admission to a G&T program. In a country in which 80% of school teachers are white, it is likely that African American kids are systematically being underidentified for these programs.

In Chicago, the odds of being selected for a G&T program are already very small, no matter your race. In 2017, Chicago Public Schools received 11,184 applications for 1,733 seats in its selective enrollment programs; 38,438 applications came in for just 3,471 seats in magnet schools.[10]

The best schools in Chicago, such as Lincoln Elementary, are full to capacity and do not admit students from outside their attendance zone— at least not knowingly. "We also have address fraud," says Sawin. "They're often being reported by somebody else in the school. 'Hey, why was this playdate all the way over there?' The inspector general has been very busy." Yes, Sawin is saying that parents have been known to turn their children's classmates in for address fraud. We can only wonder where those kids ended up after being kicked out.

Changes to attendance zones are very controversial when they involve schools with different demographics and different achievement levels. "There's been an uproar when there are zone changes," says Sawin.

"Those Schools Are Usually Full"

"Yes, of course," says Tanya Anton about her experience in Los Angeles. "If you're zoned to a great school, then the value of your house is going to be higher. Those schools are usually full."[11]

That can lead to contentious situations. "Attendance zones change," Anton says, "when families pour into the attendance zone of a well-regarded school. People will pay that premium [in housing price] for what they perceive as a 10 school because of its rating on GreatSchools." But she questions that kind of decision-making. Is it right, she asks, "to base your whole housing situation on a dot on a map and a school that is rated a 10? I try to educate families to look deeper than that one number."

She admits that the system can encourage corruption. "When human beings are involved with waitlists, there's always the potential for problems," says Anton. "Some of the principals are 'pay-to-play.'" While there haven't yet been any public scandals in Los Angeles about public-school waiting lists, Los Angeles parents share anecdotes that suggest that school staff—just like their New York counterparts—have significant discretion over who gets in and who is left out of a school that is full.

Tanya Anton says that the whole system contributes to the social divisions in our society. "We're segregated by race and class," she says. "Attendance zones definitely exacerbate that."

The Price of Public School? Up to $300,000

Remember those angry parents in Philadelphia? These are the parents who bought a house in the "catchment area" of high-performing Penn Alexander and then later learned that the school was full, so their kids would very likely be sent somewhere else.

> "I for one need to start saving money… for not only did we pay a lot for our house… but in a few years we may also need money for private school. I feel we did not get what we paid for."[12]

> "Not everyone in the catchment is well off. There are poor families living here, we sacrifice a great deal to afford these overpriced apartments just so our kids can get a good education."[13]

It's worth stating again that many Americans believe that it's simply common sense that you've got to pay extra for a house in order to get your kids into the right elementary school. Even the reporter on the Philadelphia story acknowledges that people seem to pay more for their house if it comes with an enrollment preference at Penn Alexander: "Everyone knows about the catchment premium on houses within the boundaries (sometimes speculated to be as much as $100,000)."[14]

But is there really a price premium for attendance zones?

As it turns out, this isn't just neighborhood gossip. Numerous economic studies have shown that people pay far more money for homes that come with a neighborhood school with higher test scores. One study in Massachusetts showed that test scores 5% higher than a neighboring school resulted in a 2% price premium for local houses.[15] A later study found that the extra cost for such a school is more likely to be closer to 10%.[16] In cities like Los Angeles and New York, that would mean that families are paying $100,000 or more just to gain access to specific coveted "public" schools.

On the ground, there is some evidence that the highest-performing schools have an even more dramatic distortionary impact on housing prices. Tanya Anton, the public-school consultant in Los Angeles, says that some parents are willing to pay up to $300,000 more to buy a house in the "right" attendance zone in Los Angeles. "And if you're looking for a two-bedroom apartment within the attendance zone of the Carpenter school," she told a group of parents in 2016, "you're going to pay an extra $1,000 per month."

It's hard to overstate the importance of this. It means that most working-class families simply can't compete for access to these schools. Jacqueline Tager, a Los Angeles real estate agent with Sotheby's, tells me that the price premium is going up. She says that houses zoned for Ivanhoe Elementary in the Silver Lake neighborhood of Los Angeles used to sell for about $100,000 more. Now it's "probably $150,000 to $200,000."[17]

But housing prices don't just go up for families with young children. Prices go up for all of us.

Let's say that you and your spouse—with no kids and no plans to have kids—want to move to Silver Lake. You hope to find a hillside home with a view of the beautiful Silver Lake Reservoir. Well, you'd better start saving up. All the homes within view of the reservoir are zoned for Ivanhoe. You and your spouse will therefore be competing with families who are paying not just for the house with a view but also for access to the school. Maybe you're willing to pay $150,000 extra to get the house you want. Or maybe you can't afford that, and you'll just have to look for someplace else to live.

The Address Cops

In urban and suburban areas, address fraud is rampant. If you are a middle-class or working-class family, you will almost certainly be able to find a better school for your children by lying about your address.

The moral lines are blurry. Is it okay to keep your kids in a school they love, after you've moved out of the zone or the district? If you get divorced, can you use the address of the noncustodial parent? Is it a form of civil disobedience to lie about your address in order to get your child out of a school that is racially and socioeconomically isolated due to the placement of attendance-zone boundaries?

School authorities often take a hard line with parents who try to make the system work for them. Just outside of Columbus, Ohio, the Dublin City Schools district doesn't have any sympathy for families who move outside the district when the kids are midway through a school. Deputy Superintendent Tracey Miller says, "I am surprised when a parent decides to move, let's say, the student's junior year. They cannot understand why the school system couldn't let their student finish out their junior or senior year. But, we can't [let them do that]."[18]

A surprising number of districts and schools are known to hire investigators to sniff out the "cheaters." It's happened in New York, New Jersey,

Ohio, California, Illinois, the District of Columbia, and many other places. In San Francisco, Boston, and Beverly Hills, the districts have set up anonymous hotlines for parents to inform on other parents. San Francisco calls it their "Residency Fraud Reporting" program: "The district has installed an Address Tipline to accept reports of suspected address fraud. You may make a confidential report by calling (415) 522-6783 or by e-mailing information to AddressTipline@sfusd.edu."[19] In Beverly Hills, inspector Robin Reid proudly tells the *Los Angeles Times* that he "stakes out homes and follows students to and from school."[20]

While many districts will simply expel the child from school, other districts have prosecuted or sued parents. At least sixteen states have laws that officially make it a felony or a misdemeanor to lie about your address in order to enroll your child in a school. States such as New York will occasionally prosecute parents using general antilarceny or antifraud statutes. And sometimes a school district—as a government entity—will pass punitive measures of their own, such as Administrative Regulation 5111.1, which was passed by the board of education in Beverly Hills in 2014.[21] It allows district staff to assess punitive fines on parents who lie about their address. At $150 a day, an offending parent could be fined up to $27,000 per child who attended for a full year, which is significantly more than the $16,695 that the district spent per student in 2018–2019.[22]

Every year, the inspector general for the Chicago Board of Education publishes an annual report that summarizes the results of address investigations in the Chicago Public Schools.[23] And every year, the report recommends that out-of-district parents be sued for hundreds of thousands of dollars for illegally accessing the city's schools. Other parents are punished for lying about their address within the district in order to gain a better shot at gaining entry into one of Chicago's sought-after Selective Enrollment schools. Ironically, these parents are lying about living in *poorer* neighborhoods, because the Selective Enrollment schools ease their strict enrollment requirements for residents of lower-income neighborhoods.[24]

So, in Chicago, sometimes you can get your child into a better school by falsely claiming that you live in an *affluent* area. In other cases, she can get into a better school if you falsely claim that you live in a *low-income* neighborhood. Chicago parents have quite a task in figuring out where the district wants them to live.

"Identifiable Photos of Children"

Phillip Becnel spies on schoolchildren for a living.

Becnel is a private investigator whose firm is often hired to conduct live surveillance of public-school students in order to determine whether they live where their parents say they live. In Washington DC, for example, Becnel's firm was tapped by the DC Public Schools to stake out popular charter schools in an effort to catch suburban families who have lied about their addresses.

The typical challenges of a normal investigation, says Becnel, "are enhanced when it comes to doing surveillance on children." He writes in *Fraud Magazine*:

> For example, during the colder months when it's darker in the mornings it can be very difficult to get identifiable photographs of children because they often wear coats with hoods. Our firm often uses video with night vision in colder months, and we use software that enhances facial features.
>
> Also, neighbors and subjects, of course, are suspicious when they might see people taking photos of children. Therefore, we've found that female investigators are better suited for surveillance that takes place near schools because women tend to raise less eyebrows.[25]

However creepy it may seem, Becnel and his colleagues are not breaking the law. His firm is fulfilling a function—conducting district residency checks—that was explicitly allowed by the US Supreme Court in 1983.[26] More about this in Chapter Ten.

In other places, enforcement falls to teachers and principals.

Carpenter Community Charter is a high-performing school in the charming upscale neighborhood of Studio City in Los Angeles. In the past, up to 10% of the students at Carpenter used fake addresses to enroll.[27] Most charter schools in California are forbidden from establishing an attendance zone, so any family in the district is eligible to enter the lottery for enrollment. But not at Carpenter. If a traditional public school *converts* to charter status, as Carpenter did, that school is required to give enrollment preferences to students living in the former attendance zone of the school.

"I totally get why people would do anything to get their child into Carpenter," Principal Joseph Martinez told the *Los Angeles Times*.[28] The school has some of the highest test scores of any elementary school in the Los Angeles Unified School District, as well as enrichment classes that would be the envy of many private schools.

The school has contracted with a private company to analyze the addresses provided by students in an effort to identify what the *Times* calls "cheaters." In Carpenter's case, Principal Martinez himself did the home checks. "My heart does go out to those kids," Martinez told the *Times*. "But I have to put the higher priority on people who have not broken the law. Their parents have put them in this predicament that will disrupt their education."

"Hey, Where's Your Toothbrush At?"

I was able to speak to one young woman—I'll call her Melissa—who conducts "home verification" checks for a medium-sized district in California. For newly enrolled kids in middle school and high school, she says "we have to verify their address." About 10% of the home checks reveal that the family was lying about their address. Approximately 5%–7% of the checks are inconclusive: "We know they don't live there, but we can't prove it."[29]

It isn't glamorous work. "I go knock on the door," says Melissa. "'Does such and such live here?'" Often the family will try to use a doctored utility bill to claim residency. "They just copy-and-paste their name on the bill."

At other times, Melissa will have to investigate a homeless family. "We're making sure that they're homeless in [our district]" and not somewhere else, she says. "I'll do a home verification for a family living in a car. They just tell me where they park the car." And some more privileged families will *claim* to be homeless just to get access to a desirable school.

Even the truly homeless are prevented from enrolling in district schools if their "address" isn't right. One homeless family lost access to their school when they finally found housing in a neighboring community. Not willing to uproot her kids from the school they loved, the mom was willing to return to homelessness in order to keep her kids enrolled. "She was ready to give up her housing," remembers Melissa with astonishment, "just so her kids could go back to the same school." But the district wouldn't let her do it. The kids were kicked out.

Melissa reports that the home checks can be uncomfortable. Many of the parents will try to stick to their lie, even when presented with evidence that they used a fraudulent address. "Kids are the most honest," she says. "I ask them to show me their clothes. 'Hey, where's your toothbrush at?'"

Bart Simpson Escapes from Springfield

Lying about your address to get into a decent school is so common that it has leaked into popular culture. On the 1990s Aaron Spelling drama *Beverly Hills, 90210*, the middle-class nerd Andrea Zuckerman illegally uses her grandmother's address so that she can escape her Van Nuys high school and enroll in fictional West Beverly High. And in a 2009 episode of *The Simpsons*, Marge and Homer rent a fake apartment in order to get their kids into the coveted "Waverly Hills" school district. The episode is titled "9-0-2-1-D'oh!"

The media love these unsettling stories about address fraud and enforcement. But most journalists have been reluctant to stare at the issue straight on and ask how and why the laws work this way. They've ignored the underlying causes and the political forces that have shaped the system.

Chapter 7
Simple, Fair, and Open

New York Mayor Bill de Blasio says there's not much that can be done about the patterns of racial separation in the city's public schools. "You have to respect families," he says, "who have made a decision to live in a certain area oftentimes because of a specific school." The parents, he notes, have "made massive life decisions and investments because of which school their kid would go to."[1]

He doesn't say it out loud, but de Blasio is implicitly endorsing a system of state-sponsored discrimination. In order to respect (protect?) those parents who've bought their way into the attendance zones of the best schools, other families need to be kept out. Attendance-zone boundaries do that. De Blasio appointed Carmen Fariña as his first schools chancellor, and she agreed. "I want to see diversity in schools organically," Fariña told a town hall meeting in 2016. "I don't want to see mandates."[2]

Fariña implies that the racial divisions and inequality in the New York schools have emerged "organically." But, as we've seen, that's not the case. Richard Rothstein demonstrated, in his book *The Color of Law*, that the residential segregation of American cities was not *accidental*, driven primarily by the uncoordinated actions of millions of individuals. Instead, segregation was largely dictated by law and government policies that sorted families by race. So, too, are the racial and social divisions in our schools driven by misguided government policies that sort kids into different schools depending on where they live.

With the backing of state law, school districts grant enrollment preferences based on geography. They then discriminate against kids who live on the wrong side of the line, preventing them from gaining equal access to a school that might be just down the road. And then savvy parents lie about their address. Or they use their financial means to get onto the right side of the line, bidding up homes in the preferred zone. The real estate market is then forever distorted in ways that encourage ever-greater inequality, as well as divisions along race and class lines.

De Blasio and Fariña are arguing against forced integration. They don't want kids to be assigned to schools outside the neighborhood. Fair enough. Many parents—black and white, rich and poor—have resisted student assignment plans that force their children to endure long bus rides to get to a faraway school.

Kamala Harris, in the first Democratic debate of 2019, excoriated Joe Biden for his opposition to federally mandated "busing." But soon after the debate, Harris released a statement saying that she believes busing should be "in the toolbox" and not mandated by the courts or Congress. Note that—for all the controversy—Biden and Harris basically agree that district officials have every right to assign kids to faraway schools in order to combat racial segregation. I've been unable to find any evidence that Biden or Harris have ever challenged the policies that sort children within the same neighborhood into elite or failing schools based on whether the children live on one side of the street or the other.

The Perversity of School Assignment

Why are children being assigned to schools at all? Why do we trust this incredibly important decision to a government official? We aren't assigned to a doctor by the government. Or a hospital. We aren't assigned where to live (although, as I discussed in Chapter Three, the government tried that until it was made illegal). We certainly aren't assigned a grocery store. But our children are "assigned" to a school when they are five years old. And many lower-income kids, of all races, find themselves assigned to dysfunctional failing schools with abysmal records of student performance.

Shouldn't any parent be reluctant to turn their children over to these assigned schools? The folks in charge of student assignment at your local school district, however well intentioned, don't have any idea that your daughter is dyslexic and loves to dance. When they assign your son to a school, they don't take into account his aptitude for science or his difficulty in regulating his emotions.

I wonder what would happen if more American families refused to settle for the school they've been assigned to. We spend hours looking at online reviews before forking over $800 for a new refrigerator. In my house, the simple choice of a Saturday night restaurant often requires forty-five minutes of research on Yelp, Chowhound, and Eater LA. Isn't it a core duty of any parent to find the best available school option for their children? Aside from love, health, and safety, what could be more important?

Yet more than half of American parents, of all races and income levels, just send their kids to the school assigned to them by school-district officials.

I have great sympathy for these parents. It's not easy to buy a house in a neighborhood where the prices are inflated because of the assigned school. It's not easy to navigate the bureaucracy that enables your child to escape her assigned school. It's certainly not easy to pay for private school or to homeschool your children.

But the kids deserve more. Every American parent should be making an active choice about where their children will be educated.

To help parents with these difficult decisions, the process of applying to public schools should be simple, fair, and open. State laws should remove those barriers that prevent families from finding and accessing the schools that will be the best for their children. Removing those barriers should start with forbidding school-district officials from assigning kids to schools based on which side of the street they live on.

Mayor de Blasio acknowledges that geographical school assignment leads to more inequality and creates racial and social divisions in our schools. But—get this—he wants *more* poor children to attend the school they've been assigned to. He has been accused of "trying to kill" charter schools in New York City,[3] which are often the primary escape route for many families who've been geographically assigned to failing schools. In 2019, at a candidate forum hosted by the National Education Association, he said that one of his primary goals, if elected president, would be to "get away from charter schools."[4]

De Blasio is openly hostile to public school choice. What he doesn't say openly is that, in the absence of choice, what he supports is *school assignment*. More specifically, because he wants to keep attendance zones and enrollment preferences, he favors *geographic school assignment*.

There are a handful of districts around the country that have eliminated or de-emphasized attendance zones, including Boston,[5] Berkeley,[6] Buffalo,[7] DC,[8] Hartford,[9] New Orleans,[10] and San Francisco.[11] But all of these districts have implemented a centralized system called Controlled Choice. In practice, this means that parents are asked to list a number of school preferences, then a computer program assigns kids to schools based on a wide variety of criteria.

While this has some advantages over a system dominated by attendance zones, it still relies on the government to assign children to schools. The top-down, centralized process is hidden behind a veil of computer code, and it is still subject to manipulation by powerful insiders. In Washington, DC, former chancellor Antwan Wilson got fired for improperly subverting the system and getting his teenage daughter admitted to the school of her choice that had a six-hundred-student waitlist.[12] In New Orleans, a full third of families did not get their first choice in 2018.[13] Like geographic school assignment, Controlled Choice isn't simple, isn't fair, and isn't open.

School Choice and Segregation

There's a whole genre of education writing based on the idea that "school choice" is the reason that our schools are racially segregated and unequal.

Take the news story "When School Choice Means Choosing Segregation" by Allison McCann in *VICE News*:

> The resegregation of America's public schools is due
> largely to two decades of Supreme Court rulings that
> all but ended mandatory desegregation plans, but
> it has not been helped by the growing movement
> toward school choice.[14]

Or take the opinion piece "School Choice Is the Enemy of Justice" by
Erin Aubry Kaplan in the *New York Times*:

> Black and brown students have more or less resegre-
> gated within charters, the very institutions that prom-
> ised to equalize education.[15]

Or look at the academic white paper produced by the UCLA Civil
Rights Project, *Choice without Equity: Charter School Segregation and the
Need for Civil Rights Standards*:

> As the country moves steadily toward greater segrega-
> tion and inequality of education for students of color
> in schools with lower achievement and graduation
> rates, the rapid growth of charter schools has been
> expanding a sector that is even more segregated than
> the public schools.[16]

Sounds damning, doesn't it?

This way of thinking is even built into the California Education Code.
In order to be granted a charter by a school district, the charter school
founders have to identify "the means by which the school will achieve a
racial and ethnic balance among its pupils that is reflective of the general
population."[17]

The California State Legislature, like the education writers cited earlier, chooses to ignore the fact that 78% of public-school children attend their assigned public school.[18] If American public schools are divided along economic and racial lines (and it's indisputable that they are), then *it is primarily because of school assignment policies*, not because a minority of parents look for better public-school options for their children.

The best traditional public school in our neighborhood, Mount Washington Elementary, serves a population that is 59% white, while all seven of the surrounding schools have white populations of 9% or lower. Is Mount Washington Elementary required by the Education Code to maintain a student population that is "reflective of the general population"? No.

In 2019, a group of researchers from the Urban Institute released the first major study of school choice and segregation. They discovered that charter schools have two effects on the racial divisions between schools, and the two effects offset each other. On the one hand, increasing charter school enrollment did lead to more racially divided schools within the district, but the effect was slight (a 1 percentage point increase in the number of students attending charter schools corresponded to an increase in segregation by 0.1 percentage points). On the other hand, they found that *cross-district* segregation was *reduced* by increasing enrollment in charter schools. In large metropolitan areas, they found the net impact of the two forces to be very close to zero.[19]

Let's just review this one more time: Poor kids are excluded—by state law and district policy—from gaining fair access to the best public schools. Those poor kids are disproportionately black and Hispanic (though, by raw numbers, they are also majority white). Then, when those poor families go out and look for other options besides the failing, segregated local school they've been assigned to, we cry "Segregation!" We criticize the very policy that gave them control over their own destiny.

To me it seems obtuse. Perhaps fewer families would choose charter schools if they had equal access to the best public schools in their communities.

The Urban Institute researchers put it this way:

> Patterns resulting from black and Hispanic families
> choosing schools that they feel meet their children's
> needs should not be interpreted with the same lens
> as the government-mandated segregation that was
> outlawed by the US Supreme Court in *Brown v. Board
> of Education.*[20]

It is geographic school assignment, not public school choice, that is primarily responsible for the racial divisions in our schools. If you want to break down the racial and social divisions in our schools, that's the first place to look.

Simple, Fair, and Open

We already have a simple, fair, and open process for families to enroll in public schools—lotteries. Charter schools hold lotteries for enrollment spots when the number of applying students exceeds the number of available seats. In most states, these lotteries are mandated by law. And charter schools are forbidden from excluding you based on where you live within the school district. This is precisely because a school might be inclined to restrict its enrollment to a specific set of families by using a geographic boundary to carve out its desired population. Charter schools are forbidden from doing this because they are public schools and therefore must be open to the public.

Other public schools use lotteries, too. As discussed in Chapter Four, California districts that choose to participate in the Districts of Choice program must use a lottery to allocate scarce available seats. In Los Angeles, some special district programs, like dual language immersion programs, use random lotteries if there are more applicants than spots. Millions of public-school families participate in such enrollment lotteries every year in the US.

Tanya Anton, the Los Angeles school admissions consultant introduced in Chapter Six, says that school-based lotteries provide fewer opportunities for shenanigans than enrollment systems run by the district. "If the lottery is public and it's a charter school," she says, "there's really no way to fudge it."[21]

There's no doubt that some unscrupulous charter schools try to manipulate the makeup of their student population in order to increase test scores or maintain a more homogenous student body. It isn't right, but it happens. But, as we've seen, it also happens in the traditional public schools. At least charter schools are breaking the law when they engage in such conduct. By contrast, the law *provides cover* for traditional public schools that aim to control who gets in by using attendance zones or selective enrollment criteria (such as a gifted-and-talented program).

What should be clear by now is that our current system is not fully open and does not provide equal access to everyone. It isn't a fair system. And it seems to cut against some of the core principles of our society, including the idea that everyone should be treated equally under the law.

Imagine a world in which every public school was open to applications from the public and was required to hold a lottery to determine who would be admitted. In such a world, parents wouldn't have to play the games they play today, making gut-wrenching decisions about real estate and housing in order to do what's right for their children.

Critics will argue that a fully open system would be unworkable. How would a district plan from year to year, if any student could go to any school? But there are ways to make it workable. I was discussing this issue with Tony Miller, former Deputy Secretary of Education under President Obama, and he suggested that simple guidelines could alleviate potential logistical issues. For example, a school district could provide transportation to any school within a five-mile radius of a student's home. Other district schools would be open to that student, but her family would have to arrange for transportation— perhaps partially subsidized by the district— for those more distant schools.

Such a system will not make all the problems of our education system go away. There are too few good schools. As a parent, it's not always easy to figure out which school might be best for your child. And there are always trade-offs—Is it better for my child to go to a small school where she'll get lots of attention? Or a large school that has more opportunities? Will she do best in a school where all of the students are affluent and academically advanced? Or will it be better for her social and emotional development if she is exposed to all sorts of different people? There may be no clear right or wrong answer to any of these questions.

In a world of open public schools, families will sort themselves based on what they think is most important. Some of them will make mistakes. Perhaps we will learn from one another's mistakes. And perhaps the schools will slowly become better over time. This is how we make all the other difficult decisions in our lives—for example, choosing a doctor or a hospital.

For those who support the current system of geographic school assignment, there are a number of questions: Are you comfortable with one city street, say North Avenue in Chicago, determining whether a given child will be able to read by the end of eighth grade or not? Are you comfortable with the racial and social divisions of Lincoln Elementary and Manierre Elementary, two schools that serve the same neighborhood? Are you comfortable with laws and policies that cause thousands of American families to lie about where they live? Are you comfortable with the artificially inflated cost of housing in these neighborhoods?

I'm not comfortable with any of it.

PART III: LOCATION, LOCATION, ADJUDICATION

Chapter 8

Unlocking the Gates of Opportunity

What I love about this story is that it captures, in microcosm, the paradox that lies at the heart of democracy.

You've got high-minded ideals, as reflected in the founding documents of our democratic institutions. Due process! Equal protection of the law! High-quality public schools that are open to all! These are the promises that politicians need to make in order to galvanize the public's support for the creation of institutions that have tremendous power over the people.

But, from the very beginning, the politicians find themselves pushed and pulled by special interests who have political power. These folks want to make sure that they get their fair share of government resources—or perhaps more than their fair share. They push hard for policies that give them preferential access to governmental rights and resources.

Over time, government policies and programs drift away from the principles of our founding, but the politicians never stop talking about those ideals. Indeed, you could argue that an equilibrium develops over time: In a democratic country like ours, some of the most abiding government policies are those that appear on the surface to be equal and fair (neighborhood schools!) but that allow a politically powerful constituency to capture a nominally public resource. That constituency then puts more and more of their political support, including money, behind the politicians who protect and support the unfair handout.

Call this phenomenon the "Bleeding Heart and the Robber Baron."

You see it over and over in areas of public policy meant to promote equitable health and welfare. During the housing boom of the early 2000s,

Republicans and Democrats both extolled the benefits of home owner-ship, expanding government-sponsored loan programs like Fannie Mae and Freddie Mac that allowed lower-income people greater access to mortgages. Politicians taking credit for helping working-class Americans buy homes? The Bleeding Hearts.

With Congress encouraging Fannie Mae and Freddie Mac to loosen their lending standards, Americans were able to take out more federally approved mortgage loans. Never mind that the homes were of dubious value and the debt was excessive. Brokers and lenders making billions of dollars on bad loans guaranteed by the government? The Robber Barons.

Or look at the ongoing student loan crisis. Bleeding-heart politicians of both parties bemoan the high cost of college and create massive student aid programs to help middle-class kids go to college. Seeing this huge influx of cheap capital into the hands of students, the universities (both private and public, for-profit and nonprofit) are positioned to be the Robber Barons. They raise tuition and other costs, enriching themselves while many students drown in debt for degrees that are never completed or that have little value in the job market.

Health care too. Expressing compassion and concern for the uninsured, politicians pass a law requiring people to buy health insurance. Then the stock-market valuation of your favorite health insurance company goes up by a billion dollars or more.[1]

The phenomenon of the Bleeding Heart and the Robber Baron depends on the public's wishful thinking. Government aid for college tuition is one of the least controversial policies in America and is enthu-siastically supported by the vast majority of Democrats, Republicans, and independents. The public often fails to consider the possibility that the economic benefit is unlikely to flow to the beneficiaries of the program and will instead go to a small group of powerful insiders. But this happens over and over again.

You probably haven't heard of the Bleeding Heart and the Robber Baron before (because I just coined the term). But you may have heard of an analogous concept, the Baptist and the Bootlegger. The economist Bruce Yandle first identified this phenomenon:

> The theory's name is meant to evoke 19th century laws banning alcohol sales on Sundays. Baptists supported Sunday closing laws for moral and religious reasons, while bootleggers were eager to stifle their legal competition. Thus, politicians were able to pose as acting in the interests of public morality, even while taking contributions from bootleggers. . . . Such a coalition makes it easier for politicians to favor both groups. . . . The Baptists lower the costs of favor-seeking for the bootleggers, because politicians can pose as being motivated purely by the public interest even while they promote the interests of well-funded businesses. . . . [Baptists] take the moral high ground, while the bootleggers persuade the politicians quietly, behind closed doors.[2]

It may seem surprising that moonshiners and bootleggers would want to outlaw some alcohol sales—until you realize that *the existing producers benefit from restrictions on other would-be suppliers.*

The alliance of the Bleeding Heart and the Robber Baron parallels the ill-matched Baptist and the Bootlegger coalition. The high-minded ideals, instead of coming from the religious right, are touted by left-leaning Bleeding Hearts who propose a big new government program to make health care, housing, or education more affordable or accessible. The Robber Barons, instead of looking for protection from competitors as the Bootleggers did, look to capture the spigot of monetary benefits established by the government program. In many cases, the Robber Barons are large multinational companies, such as pharmaceutical companies, the big mortgage lenders, or private, for-profit universities. But the Robber

Barons might also take the form of large nonprofits—elite universities, nonprofit hospitals, public sector unions.

And don't underestimate the possibility that the Robber Barons might be your neighbors who picked their home because it gave their children preferential access to a special public school.

The Intent of the State Legislature

Through the mid-1980s, California had a community college system that was carved up into districts, much as the K–12 education system is today. Your address determined which community college you could attend (and which you couldn't).

But in 1987, the state decided to reform the community college system to combat enrollment declines that began in the 1960s. The goal was to improve the academic program and reinvent the system as a feeder of transfers to the Cal State and University of California systems. One goal was to make the community colleges more appealing to students. The governor set up a commission that, among other things, recommended ending geographic assignment of students to community colleges.[3]

The California legislature agreed and added the following provision to the Education Code:

> It is not in the best interests of the people of the State
> of California that attendance at a community college
> be restricted to a person's district of residence. It is
> the intent of the Legislature in enacting this article to
> provide for the unrestricted enrollment and atten-
> dance of students at community colleges, thereby
> providing each resident of the state an equal oppor-
> tunity to attend the community college of his or her
> choice.[4]

Before I turn to look at how the courts might view geographic enroll-ment preferences in K–12 education, I want to imagine what kind of legislative solutions might address some of the problems that I've discussed. California community colleges were once closed institutions serving geographically isolated communities. But the California legislature took action that changed the enrollment policy for these institutions and made them fully open to the public.

Since 1987, California students have been able to choose which community college they attend. My wife, Simone, is a great example. After we got married, she decided to go back to school to become an occupational therapist, and she needed prerequisite courses before she could even apply to a master's degree program at a university. She was able to apply to several local community colleges, including Los Angeles (where we live) and Glendale (where we don't). She shopped around for the right combination of courses and also looked for the best professors, ultimately taking courses at both schools.

One can imagine a similar statute, in any of the fifty states, that would open up K–12 schools with a declaration like this:

> It is not in the best interests of the people of the State that attendance at a public school be restricted to a person's district of residence or attendance zone. It is the intent of the Legislature in enacting this article to provide for the unrestricted enrollment and attendance of students at public schools, thereby providing each child of the state an equal opportunity to attend the public school of his or her family's choice.

The problem, of course, is that such a law would likely face a significant obstacle in the objections of affluent homeowners who have preferential access to the elite public schools in the current system. It would also likely face opposition from powerful political leaders and unions who benefit from the status quo. But public-school enrollment is projected to continue to decline in many states over the next decade, so perhaps

one or more states may be forced to consider such a move. K–12 enrollment in California, for example, is projected to drop 7% by 2027 (from
its peak in 2005).[5]

If you squint your eyes hard enough, you might even be able to
imagine the US Congress stepping in to end geographic enrollment
preferences. Something similar happened in the 1950s and 1960s when
Congress passed a wave of civil rights laws that attempted to end racial
discrimination in key spheres of American life. These included the Civil
Rights Act of 1957 (voting), the Civil Rights Act of 1964 (employment,
voting, and access to public facilities), the Voting Rights Act of 1965
(voting), and the Fair Housing Act of 1968 (home ownership and renting).
These laws passed at the federal level precisely because state and local
policies had been co-opted by special interests (white citizens) in order
to protect their own access to rights and resources.

Redlining in the housing and mortgage markets was itself outlawed via
the Community Reinvestment Act of 1977.[6] Because Congress once used
a federal statute to prohibit federal agencies and banks from discriminating
against certain neighborhoods in the issuance of mortgages, isn't it possible
to imagine that Congress might one day use a federal statute to prohibit
schools from discriminating against certain neighborhoods?

An Educational Civil Rights Act for the twenty-first century would
forbid any local education agency (LEA) from using a person's residential
address within the LEA as a disqualifying factor for admission to any of
the district's schools. (*Local education agency* is the technical legal term for
a school district.) If concerns about federalism and local control prevent
Congress from outlawing this type of discrimination outright, then it
could condition the receipt of federal education funding on such policies.
In fact, this "strings attached" approach is the primary way that federal
education policy is implemented today.

Such a law wouldn't abolish the jurisdictional lines around school
districts, but it would prevent a school district from using its administrative power to draw arbitrary lines of access around its best public schools.

It would put the "open" back in "open enrollment" and would force overenrolled schools to hold lotteries for admissions (as charter schools, and some other public schools, are currently required to do).

In theory, such a law could appeal to Democrats as a way to end government-sponsored policies that encourage and perpetuate social divisions of class and race. Some Republicans might see it as a way to advance the cause of school choice, dramatically increasing public school choice across all fifty states overnight.

Similarly, at the state level, a state legislature could require districts to open up every district school to all the residents in that district (and end the geographic preferences). This would bring enrollment laws into alignment with the original promise of public education, as outlined in all fifty state constitutions. As I discussed in Chapter One, the specific language of the promise varies quite a bit by state. But there is no question that the original idea of public or common schools is that they would be "general" or "open to all" and that they could not be captured by any interest groups, however wealthy and powerful.

Perhaps the simplest and most elegant solution would have a state legislature extend successful enrollment processes used by charter schools to cover all public schools in the state. Every public school—not just charters—would then have to accept all comers and implement a fair, unbiased lottery if enrollment exceeds the number of available spaces.

On a personal level, we should all have sympathy for the people who would oppose such reforms. Take a family who has purchased a home in a sought-after attendance zone, paying $200,000 more for access to that public school. Those parents were attempting to secure the best education for their children, and that's always a laudable goal. But that doesn't mean we should continue to block open access to these public schools. Bad policies need to be changed. Especially when they are being used to capture public services for private gain.

In many ways, these people are like the taxi companies in New York City. Taxi companies paid exorbitant prices, up to millions of dollars, for taxicab medallions that would allow them to operate taxis within the city limits. For years, these medallion owners fought off efforts to issue more medallions—and improve taxi service for millions of New Yorkers—because they wanted to be protected from the competition. With the emergence of ride-sharing services such as Uber and Lyft, the medallions have become almost worthless. And taxi companies have tried to use their lobbying power to block such services and retain their protected position.

But the courts have said no. Buying a taxi medallion does not mean that you are protected from disruptive competition until the end of time. Likewise, buying a house that gives you preferential access to a public school does not mean that you will be able to keep other families out forever.

In practice, of course, lawmakers might find it difficult to pass a law that would cut against the interests of homeowners, who wield political clout, as well as the corporate investors who have amassed thousands of single-family homes in California and other states.

The laws may change. Or maybe the courts will step in.

Challenging Attendance Zones in the Courts

In the following chapters, I want to focus on the legal status of geographic attendance zones. To my eye, attendance zones clearly violate laws—including constitutional promises—that protect us all from arbitrary and unjust discrimination.

I am making four specific claims:

1. **In states where education has been recognized as a "fundamental right," geographic attendance zones violate promises of the equal protection of the law.** Thirteen states recognize education as a fundamental right, and attendance zones are vulnerable to challenge in these states. When fundamental rights are implicated, the courts are required to apply strict scrutiny to any laws or policies that constrain that

right, requiring the government to prove that the restriction
serves a "compelling government interest" and that the
policy has been "narrowly tailored." Attendance zones are
likely to fail these tests.

2.   **Where the state promises that public schools will be
     "open to all," attendance-zone boundaries and geographic
     enrollment preferences are inconsistent with that promise.**
     In some states, the law requires the legislature to create public
     schools that are "open to all" children or that provide "equal
     educational opportunity." Attendance-zone boundaries,
     which effectively exclude the vast majority of children from
     attending the best public schools, are inconsistent with these
     requirements. This group includes fourteen states, three of
     which also recognize education as a fundamental right.

3.   **The promise of "equal protection" in the Fourteenth
     Amendment of the US Constitution—properly interpreted—
     does not allow public-school districts to categorize district
     families by their address and use that categorization to
     make discriminatory judgments about who is or isn't
     eligible to enroll in a specific school.** Because education has
     been judged to be an "important governmental interest," the
     courts cannot simply take a deferential stance toward state
     laws and district policies that are so egregiously arbitrary and
     discriminatory. Some heightened form of judicial scrutiny
     is warranted, and attendance-zone boundaries are highly
     vulnerable under such scrutiny.

4.   **Current attendance-zone boundaries are not compliant
     with a federal civil rights law that prohibits the use of
     such boundaries if they worsen segregation.** A little-
     known statute from the 1970s—the Equal Educational

Opportunities Act of 1974—prohibits the assignment of
a minority child to a school that is not the nearest school
to her home, if doing so exacerbates existing segregation.
Attendance-zone boundaries, as currently drawn, violate
this prohibition and can be challenged by individual students
who have been assigned to schools that are not the nearest to
their home.

We're treading new ground here, because many of these issues have not yet been brought to the courts in a way that forces the judges to rule yea or nay. What we do know is that the courts have often been very skeptical when the government sets up an institution of public education for a given jurisdiction and then excludes a particular category of people from enrolling.

That skepticism was on display in the famous *Plyler v. Doe* case that the US Supreme Court considered in 1982, when the judges struck down a Texas law that prohibited undocumented immigrants from enrolling in the public schools.[7] That skepticism made another appearance in 1995 when the US Supreme Court ruled that Virginia could not categorically exclude Virginia women from attending the Virginia Military Institute. In *United States v. Virginia*, Ruth Bader Ginsburg wrote for the majority and declared that such an exclusion is a violation of the Equal Protection Clause of the Fourteenth Amendment. She added that particular scrutiny of governmental policy is warranted when "state actors [control] the gates of opportunity."[8]

Not one of the four legal issues I'm posing is a Slam Dunk Yes for the courts. But neither is any of them a Door Slam No. By looking closely at each claim, we'll learn a lot about how our courts manage the balance between the ideals and the realities of democracy.

Chapter 9

Open to All?

———————

A couple of months ago, I was browsing through an obscure education policy book called *School Money Trials*. Published in 2007, the book compiles a number of academic articles exploring the history of state-level legal challenges to funding models for the K–12 schools.

The book has one chapter by the legal scholar John Eastman. Eastman expresses doubt that the state constitutions can be used effectively as a lever to increase funding for the K–12 schools. He argues that it would not be proper—and certainly not enforceable—for the state courts to require a certain level of funding in a state's public schools. But that doesn't mean that the state courts are powerless to combat the inequities of our school system. Toward the end of his chapter, Eastman drops this little nugget: "The several state constitutional mandates that public schools be open to 'all' the children of the state are ... easily and properly enforceable by the states."[1]

Ding, ding, ding!

A bell went off when I read that sentence—this is exactly what I had been thinking. There are nine states that require the public schools be "open to all," and attendance zones may be vulnerable to legal challenge in those states.

Waves of Lawsuits

The state courts have been a common venue for raising equal protection claims related to the public schools. This is partially because the federal courts have set such a high bar for such claims. But it is also because the states have promised—in their constitutions—to provide public education and therefore enjoy the primary responsibility for establishing the system to provide it. If that system isn't treating everyone equally under the law, then the state courts are in the best position to say so.

There have been several different types of such state lawsuits. First, there was a series of lawsuits related to desegregation and application of the *Brown v. Board of Education* decision at the state level. In my home state of California, for example, there was the famous case of *Jackson v. Pasadena City School District* (1963), which forbade school districts from manipulating geographic attendance zones with an explicit goal of maintaining segregation of black and white students.[2]

Next came a wave of lawsuits focused on differences in spending across districts. The pioneering case was *Serrano v. Priest* (1971), also in California.[3] This case struck down California's school funding mechanism, which relied on local property taxes and therefore led to dramatic discrepancies in per-pupil spending across districts. California's highest court ruled that education was a "fundamental right" under the California Constitution and that therefore the legislature had to equalize funding across districts to some degree. A number of other states followed suit, including New Jersey and Vermont. But similar challenges in many other states were denied by the courts. And a similar challenge in the federal courts was denied by the US Supreme Court in *San Antonio Independent School District v. Rodriguez* (1973).[4] More about this case in Chapter Ten.

Then came the "adequacy" suits of the late 1980s and early 1990s. In several states, plaintiffs filed lawsuits claiming that the state had failed to supply enough funding for adequate education of its poorest students, violating its constitutional promise to provide public education. The state courts, however, were often reluctant to step in, primarily because of the difficulty of defining what adequate funding would look like. Even when the suits were successful, as in the *Campaign for Fiscal Equity v. State of New York* (1993),[5] the rulings had little practical effect. The state briefly injected more dollars into the New York City schools, but, after the financial crisis of 2008, funding fell back to pre-lawsuit levels.

In Kentucky, the *Rose v. Council for Better Education* (1989)[6] case successfully challenged both spending disparities and the adequacy of the education budgets. That ruling did appear to result in increased funding for Kentucky's poorest districts in the years following the ruling. But claims of inadequate funding were denied by the courts in most other states, or they were resolved in other ways that had little impact on school funding.

Finally, more recent lawsuits have focused on district policies that create a high concentration of inexperienced or ineffective teachers in schools that serve poor, minority students. The pioneering case here was *Vergara v. California* (2016).[7] A Superior Court judge initially ruled that many common staffing practices by school-district officials are unconstitutional because they result in a higher proportion of ineffective teachers at schools in more impoverished areas. The plaintiffs argued that policies related to teacher tenure, dismissal restrictions, and layoff preferences violate the constitution because they have a "disparate impact"—a negative impact—on students who are poor and/or minority. But the verdict was overturned by the California Court of Appeal.[8] Suits inspired by *Vergara* have been filed in several states and are pending in New York and New Jersey.[9] The New York case was filed by Mona Davids, a fearless advocate of parents' rights and the president of the New York City Parents Union.

Thus far, as measured against their own goals, all of these efforts have failed. While *Brown* and other desegregation cases effectively ended *explicit* racial segregation, the schools remain divided along racial lines. Despite challenges to funding mechanisms, cross-district funding discrepancies remain the norm in many states. Even in places where funding has been equalized, there are still huge gaps in student performance and graduation rates, often between schools serving the same neighborhood.

I could hardly blame you if you read this history and concluded that the courts just aren't in a position to address these social divisions and inequalities.

As the legal scholar Eastman persuasively argues, the concepts of "equality" and "adequacy" do not easily submit to judicial enforcement in the realm of funding.[10] And—even where judges decide to weigh in—the judgments typically fail to have the desired effect over the long haul. What's more, the courts' approach to segregation lawsuits is naturally self-limiting: If a district can maintain schools that are divided along racial lines but avoid any mention, in official statements or documents, of an "intent" to segregate racially, then the courts are powerless to intervene. It's a get-out-of-jail-free card. Thus government policies that exacerbate the racial and economic divisions in our schools persist more than six decades after the *Brown* decision.

But maybe there's another option. Maybe there is a role for the state courts to play. Maybe they haven't yet been asked the right question.

A Question of Equal Access

Take a look at the following four questions. Which of them seem proper for the courts to take on? Which are most easily enforced through the courts? To use the technical legal term, which of these are most "justiciable"?

- Has the state legislature provided adequate funding for the public schools?

- Are differences in district funding sufficiently large to violate the principle of equal protection?

- When district policies create disparate outcomes at different schools, are the disparities so extreme that they violate the principle of equal protection?

- Is it valid for school-district officials to use race as the determining factor when deciding which children get to enroll at a school and which don't?

The last question is clearly the most justiciable. It's a simple YES or NO.

The other three questions are inherently fuzzy and would require the courts to make very difficult determinations. For example, what does "adequate" funding mean? To answer that question you would need to determine what the goal is—adequate for what? It could well have a very different meaning to different people. Or at different times in history.

Likewise, the courts will have a difficult time with questions of inequality of funding or impact. Any education policy will have different impacts on different schools and communities. Absolute equality is literally impossible, so it wouldn't be possible for the courts to mandate equality of impact. Because of this difficulty, the courts are reluctant to take cases in which there is "a lack of judicially discoverable and manageable standards for resolving the issue."[11]

But let's return to that fourth question. Access is something different. That's what *Brown v. Board of Education* was about. That case asked the simple question: Is it valid for the Topeka Board of Education to use Linda Brown's race as the determining factor when deciding that she is not allowed to enroll at Sumner Elementary?

The US Supreme Court's answer to that question was a unanimous NO.

Here's another question that is straightforward for the courts to answer: Is it valid for school officials to use a family's residential address—within the district—as the determining factor when deciding whether a child can enroll in a given school?

We don't know the answer to that question, because the courts haven't yet been asked. But the question itself is tailor-made for the role of the courts.

Imagine this: One hot August day, a bunch of kids—white, black, Hispanic, all different ages—walk to a nearby public school and try to enroll. "Nope," they're told. "This is a neighborhood school. And it's full already. You're assigned to that school over there, the failing one."

But we live in this neighborhood.

"Sorry, your house is on the wrong side of the line. This isn't your zone."

Will the courts sign off on that?

Back to the Beginning

So we find ourselves back at the state constitutions, right where we began. When the courts look to answer whether a child's address is a valid criterion to use in excluding her from enrolling in a school within her district, they will look to the state constitutions to understand the nature of the public education promise. That's where a judicial review of geographic attendance zones would begin.

You may recall from Chapter One that several state constitutions require the state legislature to establish schools that are "open to all." Those seven states are Alaska, Arizona, Indiana, New Mexico, North Dakota, South Carolina, and South Dakota. Two more states, Arkansas and Colorado, have statutory requirements that the public schools be "open to all."

This is the question for the courts in those nine states: If a school can decline to enroll a child solely based on her residential address within the district, is that school truly "open to all"?

I don't think that it is.

Similarly, five states promise "equality of educational opportunity." Louisiana, Montana, and North Carolina mention this phrase (or something very similar) in their state constitution. In Montana, for example, the state constitution says: "Equality of educational opportunity is guaranteed to each person of the state." In addition, the Supreme Court of New Jersey recognized a right to "equality of educational opportunity" in the landmark case *Robinson v. Cahill*, and the Tennessee Supreme Court did the same in *Tennessee Small School Systems v. McWherter*.[12]

When a school-district official draws a geographic attendance-zone boundary assigning a child on one side of the street to a great school and another child on the other side of the street to a failing school, it's not clear that the policy is providing the "equality of opportunity" that is promised by those five states.

But those aren't the only states where attendance-zone boundaries may be highly vulnerable. In thirteen states (including three that also have an "open to all" requirement), the courts have already declared education to be a "fundamental right." In these states, the courts are required to apply "strict scrutiny" to any classifications that create unequal access to public schools.

What's important about strict scrutiny is that it transfers the burden of proof to the government, requiring them to show that the discrimination was necessary to further a "compelling governmental interest" and that the policy was "narrowly tailored" to achieve that interest.

Such sweeping enrollment exclusions based on geography are hardly "narrowly tailored." As we've discussed before, public charter schools are forbidden from establishing geographic attendance-zone boundaries in most states. Defenders of geographic zoning would be forced to argue that the government has a "compelling interest" in setting up exclusionary boundaries for some public schools, while forbidding them for others.

These are the thirteen states in which the courts have determined education to be a fundamental right: Alabama, Arizona, California, Connecticut, Kentucky, Minnesota, New Hampshire, North Carolina, North Dakota, South Carolina, Tennessee, Virginia, West Virginia, Wisconsin, and Wyoming.

Finally, in Illinois, attendance zones of schools like Lincoln Elementary and Manierre Elementary may be vulnerable to challenge under the statutory requirement that Illinois school boards "change or revise" attendance zones in order to prevent segregation and to eliminate the "separation of children in public schools because of color, race or nationality."[13] I reviewed substantial evidence in Chapter Two that district officials in Chicago have used the Lincoln and Manierre zones to keep the children separated, rather than eliminating that separation, as required by state law.

In total I've identified a total of twenty-five states in which attendance zones may be vulnerable to legal challenge. In three of those states, the constitution contains the "open to all" or "equal educational opportunity" language, *and* the courts have ruled education to be a fundamental right: Arizona, North Carolina, and North Dakota. In these states, attendance-zone boundaries are vulnerable on two fronts, because they violate the promise that the schools be "open to all" *and* because they violate students' rights to equal protection.

The Counterarguments

This isn't the place to litigate the full legal case against geographical attendance zones drawn by school-district officials. But I do want to cover some of the counterarguments that would come up if the state courts ever consider the issue of whether attendance zones are in violation of state constitutional promises.

One key counterargument against an "open to all" challenge is that the language only requires the *system* to be open to all, not individual schools. Under this line of reasoning, a family funneled into a failing school still has access to an open public education *system*. Most state constitutions use the phrase "a system of public schools open to all" or a variation. It is unclear whether the phrase "open to all" modifies "schools" or "system." Must a school be open to all? Or just the overall system?

Arizona, in fact, is the only state that unambiguously specifies that it is the *individual school* that must be open to all families within the school district.

But the most natural meaning of that phrase, to my ear, is that the *schools* must be open to all, not just the system. If you read that language as only promising access to the overall system, then the clause is almost meaningless. For example, a state could block a student from attending any school except one specific school and then claim that the system was "open" to that student. That doesn't seem to be consistent with the spirit of the "open to all" promise. Even if the system is the unit that must be open, it's not clear that attendance zones create a system that is *sufficiently* open.

This doesn't mean that a child has a right to attend a specific school. Good public schools are scarce, especially in the inner cities. Great public schools are even harder to find. Not everyone will be able to attend the best school in the district. But, in the states discussed earlier, I believe every school district has a legal obligation to make the best schools equally accessible or equally open to all residents. A random lottery, for example, would ensure equal access while still providing the district the ability to manage enrollment across schools.

Here are potential rebuttals for some of the other likely counterarguments:

Counterargument: Even under strict scrutiny, there is no violation of state constitutional protections. Attendance zones fulfill a "compelling governmental interest" in that they place children into local schools, and the policy has been "narrowly tailored" to achieve that interest.

Rebuttal: No other public benefit or constitutionally protected right is rationed in this way. That's a powerful indicator that these broad exclusions based on your place of residence are not "narrowly tailored." In addition, attendance zones do not provide local schools for all students, because, in most states, *students are not guaranteed a spot in the school even if they live within the geographic zone.* What's more, because zones are misshapen, many children are assigned to a school that is *not* the nearest to their home.

Again, most public charter schools are forbidden from establishing a geographic attendance zone. An open lottery, like the process used by charter schools, could provide a fair and equal method of determining who can attend overenrolled schools. Other public education institutions, such as state university systems or state-funded child-care centers, do not use enrollment preferences based on your place of residence within the jurisdiction.

Counterargument: The plaintiffs have been assigned to a public school within the district, just as have students on the other side of the line. Thus they have been treated equally under the law.

Rebuttal: The children have been assigned to schools that are obviously unequal. One is failing, and the other is thriving. Equal protection requires that persons "similarly circumstanced" relative to the purpose of the law be treated equally. Two students who live on opposite sides of the same street within the boundaries of the same school district should be considered to be similarly situated relative to the purpose of public education law. The courts require that educational alternatives be "substantially comparable" if one group is allowed in and the other kept out. The schools in question are not substantially comparable.

Counterargument: The challenged statutes are a part of a "complex statutory scheme" enacted by the legislature to ensure fair and equal access to schools. Plaintiffs are improperly asking the court to insert itself into a policymaking function.

Rebuttal: This is a narrow challenge of those statutes and policies that allow for discrimination on the basis of residential address within the district. Such a case only asks whether districts are allowed to use residential address to determine who can or cannot attend a given public school, just as *Brown v. Board of Education* considered the legality of racial enrollment preferences.

Counterargument: Students already have a choice. They can choose from magnet schools, charter schools, and schools with open-enrollment seats available.

Rebuttal: This case isn't about school choice. It's about whether school officials have a right to discriminate in their enrollment decisions based on a student's residential address within the district. Because there are significant disparities in the quality of schools within the district, every child should be considered for enrollment on equal terms with all other students.

Counterargument: It's not practicable to disallow attendance zones. How will the schools determine who goes to which school?

Rebuttal: Charter schools, and other types of public schools, have demonstrated that lottery-based enrollment systems work effectively and provide a nondiscriminatory alternative. Existing law requires that charter applicants be enrolled or denied enrollment based on chance, not on their place of residence. This method has proven to be a fairer way of allocating scarce enrollment slots in high-performing public schools. Lottery-based systems do not guarantee equal outcomes, but they do guarantee equal access and equal opportunity.

Counterargument: A system of school choice will segregate the schools. Student assignment systems are needed to ensure that the schools are integrated.

Rebuttal: Although 78% of public-school students attend the neighborhood public school that they've been assigned to, our schools are still starkly divided by race and class. Indeed, the public schools are divided along racial and economic lines because *our neighborhoods* are divided on racial and economic lines. Ending geographic enrollment preferences will open up the best schools to all comers, regardless of race or class.

This case isn't about school choice. It's about whether a district has the legal right to treat its constituents differently depending on whether they live on one side of the street or the other. The US Supreme Court rightly ruled that certain school choice plans, when they led to the perpetuation of segregation, were not sufficient remedies for proven cases of intentional segregation (*Green v. County School Board of New Kent County*, 1968). But the court specifically did not disallow open-enrollment policies that permit families to have access to schools outside their neighborhood.

Counterargument: This is an issue of local control. The US Supreme Court has affirmed that states and school districts have wide latitude to implement whatever funding and student assignment policies they perceive to be best for the local community. As the court said in *Milliken v. Bradley* (1974), "No single tradition in public education is more deeply rooted than local control over the operation of schools; local autonomy has long been thought essential both to the maintenance of community concern and support for public schools and to quality of the educational process."[14]

Rebuttal: Although given much autonomy in school operations, states and districts are still bound by the promise of equal protection in the

US Constitution, as well as specific clauses of the state constitutions. The courts don't have to prescribe any particular type of student assignment system, so states and districts will still have significant flexibility to develop policies that work locally.

The narrow question is this: If a child lives within the district, can school officials use residential address to determine that child's eligibility for enrollment in the school?

Again, I don't want to imply that this case is open and shut. It's unclear how the state courts would rule on such claims. Some of the counterarguments I've discussed are serious, and it's especially difficult to overturn a policy that has such a long history.

But we should all be troubled when we see that long-standing educational policies seem to work at cross-purposes to the core constitutional promises of our democracy.

Chapter 10
Available to All on Equal Terms?

In the years after the Civil War, the Southern states passed a group of laws now known as the "Black Codes." Meant to repress and control the emancipated slaves, these laws effectively replaced the "slave codes" that similarly attempted to restrict the political and economic freedom of black people, thereby maintaining the prewar status quo. These laws restricted voting rights for African Americans, criminalized "vagrancy," and allowed for "convict lease" programs that provided cheap labor to the former plantations.

In a troubling if brilliant stroke of political irony, Southern states took their inspiration from laws passed in the *Northern* states that were opposed to slavery. Prior to the Civil War, free states such as Ohio, Illinois, Indiana, Michigan, and New York passed the first Black Code laws that aimed to discourage blacks from living there—again, by restricting their political and economic rights.[1]

Clearly, states in all regions of the US have at times been unwilling to apply the law equally and fairly. High-minded constitutional ideals occasionally give way to laws and policies that protect the politically powerful.

That's how we got the Fourteenth Amendment to the US Constitution with its promises of equal protection and due process. It is the federal government's effort to protect citizens from state laws and policies that benefit one group at the expense of another. The first section of the Fourteenth Amendment is aimed squarely at state actions that disenfranchise people within their jurisdiction: "No State shall... Nor shall any State..."

In this chapter, I examine the legal status of geographic attendance-zone boundaries in the context of the Fourteenth Amendment's promise of "the equal protection of the law" and its restrictions on state discrimination. Is it possible that school attendance zones and geographic enrollment preferences violate the Fourteenth Amendment? Or are they outside of its scope?

At first glance, it seems unlikely that the federal courts would rule that attendance zones are unconstitutional. The US Supreme Court's standard framework for analyzing equal protection claims, developed in the 1930s and 1940s, would seem to preclude them from doing so.

But the court's original definition of equal protection, outlined in the early 1900s, appears to be at odds with the geographical enrollment preferences and attendance-zone boundaries that emerged in the mid-1900s and continue to be used today. In a couple of key cases from the last thirty years, the court has shown itself to be very skeptical of policies that deny enrollment at a specific public school or university to any particular class of people within the jurisdiction.

The more liberal justices on the Supreme Court are likely to be wary of signing off on policies that keep poor, minority children from attending the best public schools in their district. There is substantial evidence that school attendance zones perpetuate and exacerbate inequality in America, separating kindergartners along class and racial lines. For these justices, a ruling that forbids district officials from drawing attendance zones could go a long way toward restoring Horace Mann's promise of public education as "the great equalizer."[2]

The liberal justices may find some unlikely allies. One of the most influential conservative jurists of the last half century, the late justice Antonin Scalia, once proposed in an opinion that the Supreme Court should abolish attendance zones. Scalia thought that guaranteeing equal access to all public schools, rather than limiting access based on geography, was the best way for the courts to apply the concept of equal protection in the context of K–12 public education.

The court is now dominated by acolytes of Scalia, and the new conservative majority may look at attendance zones with Scalia's skeptical eye. A ruling in line with Scalia's thinking would provide them an opportunity to craft a more judicially enforceable standard for the court's application of the Fourteenth Amendment in the context of K–12 school enrollment. More about Scalia and his approach in Chapter Twelve.

Let's start with how the Supreme Court has applied the principle of equal protection to the public schools in the last seventy years.

Equal Protection and the Schools

There is an extensive history of federal case law that applies the Equal Protection Clause to issues of public-school access and enrollment policies.

But, notably, the Supreme Court has not yet been asked whether it is permissible under the Fourteenth Amendment for school districts to restrict access to a given public-school based on where a student lives *within the district.* That's an open question of law.

Here's what we do know:

Can a district exclude a child from a school because of the child's race?

No. In the historic ruling in *Brown v. Board of Education* (1954),[3] the Supreme Court made it illegal for districts to segregate students into different schools by race, even if such separate schools were "equal" (which was previously allowed under the *Plessy v. Ferguson* case of 1896). In addition, the *Brown* ruling invalidated state laws—specifically in Kansas, South Carolina, Virginia, and Delaware—that required or permitted the segregation of schools by race.

Can a district operate schools that are largely divided along racial lines if there was no explicit intent to segregate students by race?

Yes. The *Milliken v. Bradley* decision in 1974[4] established that the *de facto* segregation of school districts did not violate the Constitution (distinguishing this case from the *de jure* segregation in *Brown*). A given school district cannot be subject to a court-ordered desegregation plan if there is no evidence that district officials acted with an intent to segregate the students based on their race. School segregation that is an accidental result of residential segregation is not a violation of any student's constitutional rights: "There is no claim or finding that the school district boundary lines were established with the purpose of fostering racial segregation."

Can a state establish a funding mechanism for public education that results in dramatically different levels of per-pupil funding across school districts?

Yes. The ruling in *San Antonio Independent School District v. Rodriguez* (1973)[5] declined to invalidate the funding mechanism for public education in Texas, a system that relied on local property taxes and that therefore resulted in large discrepancies in per-pupil spending between wealthy and impoverished districts. The court held that education is not a "fundamental right" under the US Constitution and that differences in wealth do not satisfy the requirements for the recognition of a "suspect class" that would require "strict scrutiny" of the laws in question. Instead, the court held that maintaining local control of the schools provides a "rational basis" for the reliance on local property taxes and that it therefore passes constitutional muster.

Can a district refuse to enroll students who are residents of the district but who do not have legal immigration status in the US?

No. *Plyler v. Doe* (1982)[6] invalidated a Texas law that withheld state educational funds for any students not "legally admitted" into the United States and that authorized school districts to deny enrollment to such children. The court held that such a law is not "rationally" related to any substantial goal of the state, especially given the potential impact on a discrete class of "innocent children" and the potential costs to the nation as a whole. More later on this case and the court's reasoning.

Can a district enforce a residency requirement by refusing to enroll students whose parents/guardians are not residents of the district?

Yes. *Martinez v. Bynum* (1983)[7] let stand a Texas law that allowed districts to refuse public-school enrollment to any students who did not have a parent or guardian who was a resident of the district. The plaintiff was a woman who allowed her brother to live with her—despite her not being his legal guardian—in order that he might gain access to the public-school system. School districts are therefore allowed to conduct residency checks to confirm that a parent or guardian lives within the jurisdictional boundaries of the district.

Can a district use a student's race to determine which public school the child will attend, even if the purpose is desegregation rather than segregation?

No. In *Parents Involved in Community Schools v. Seattle School District No. 1* (2007),[8] the court ruled that an individual student's race cannot be used as the deciding factor in school assignment. Justice Anthony Kennedy wrote for the court, "What the government is not permitted to do, absent a showing of necessity not made here, is to classify every student on the basis of race and to assign each of them to schools based on that classification."

To summarize: The court specifically allows for jurisdictional boundaries between school districts. Within a state, the court allows for funding discrepancies between those school districts. It allows for the accidental segregation of students by race within the district. But the court does *not* allow a district to actively assign students to separate schools based on race. It also does *not* allow a district to exclude resident families who do not have legal immigration status. And it does *not* allow a district to use a student's race to determine where the child goes to school. But it *does* allow a district to apply a residency requirement to confirm that the parent/guardian lives within the jurisdictional boundary of the school district, as established by law.

Again, these cases say nothing about attendance zones, which are not established by law but are drawn by local school-district officials. They don't delineate political subdivisions like the district boundaries considered in *Martinez*. Whether you live on one side of the attendance-zone boundary or the other, you are still under the jurisdiction of the same "special purpose government"—the legal definition of a school district—that was created by state law.

What type of dispute would force the federal courts to consider the constitutionality of attendance zones and geographic enrollment preferences? What would that case look like?

A Facial Challenge

The first step would be to find plaintiffs who have standing to challenge the existence of the attendance zone. This is the easy part. Take any one of the high-performing schools mentioned in Chapter Two— say, Lincoln Elementary in Chicago. Identify a group of children who live within walking distance of Lincoln but who have been assigned to Manierre Elementary, a clearly failing school also run by the Chicago Public Schools. These kids live on the wrong side of North Avenue but within the jurisdictional boundaries of the district. This distinguishes the case from *Martinez v. Bynum*, which allowed a district to require a child's parent or guardian to live within the district boundaries in order for the child to enroll.

When the children apply to enroll at Lincoln Elementary, they will be turned away, because (1) the school is full, and (2) the law gives an enrollment preference to those living on the opposite side of the boundary. Like Linda Brown's family in the 1950s, these families, once rejected, would have legal standing to challenge Lincoln's right to keep them out solely based on where they live within the jurisdictional boundaries of the Chicago Public Schools system.

The beautiful simplicity of this approach is that it challenges the constitutionality of these policies (and the laws that allow them) *on their face* (or as they are written). Such a case would not challenge how the law has been implemented (also known as an "as-applied" challenge).

In other words, such a case would not include any factual dispute. School officials cannot argue that they don't discriminate based on residential address, because they are required to do so by Illinois state law[9] and because district enrollment policies put that discrimination in writing.[10] The same would be true in many other states. Plaintiffs would not need to prove criminal intent by the school-district employees. Nor would they need to prove that such policies have a "disparate impact" on certain protected classes such as racial minorities—even though they do indeed impact these communities to a greater degree.

The goal of such a case would be to ask the federal courts whether the children in question have been denied "the equal protection of the law" promised by the Fourteenth Amendment. If the courts agree, then such laws and policies would be invalidated, and all district families would be given an equal opportunity to enroll in the school.

A Rigid Framework

At first glance, school attendance zones do not appear to be vulnerable to this type of equal protection claim under the Fourteenth Amendment. The framework that the court typically uses to evaluate such a claim requires the court to identify cases that are worthy of the court's "strict scrutiny." Under strict scrutiny, the burden is on the government to show that the law has been narrowly tailored to a "compelling government interest" that is related to the purpose of the law. If not, the law does not pass constitutional muster. It is a difficult standard to meet, and strict scrutiny often results in the invalidation of government policies that treat different classes of people differently.

But if strict scrutiny is not invoked, then the court uses a "rational basis" test to evaluate equal protection claims against the government. This is a very loose standard that asks only whether there is any conceivable rational basis for the government's discrimination. The courts are free to speculate about the purpose of a given law and the legislature's rationale. Any possible rational basis will generally do to preserve the law that's being challenged, however remote from the legislature's actual intent. The standard is so loose, in fact, that it is extremely rare for any law to be ruled unconstitutional under the rational basis test.

How do judges decide whether to apply a strict scrutiny test or a rational basis test? The Supreme Court's traditional framework requires strict scrutiny when a "fundamental right" is implicated or when a "suspect classification" is employed by the government. Fundamental rights are those recognized by the courts as deserving of special protection, either because of their importance in the Constitution or their treatment under the Due Process Clause of the Fourteenth Amendment.

A "suspect classification" is created when the government makes a distinction in its treatment of a group that has historically been subject to discrimination. Race, religion, and national origin are the only suspect classifications recognized by the federal judiciary, though other classes are recognized as "quasi-suspect" by either the federal or state courts (e.g., gender, sexual orientation, and whether you were born out of wedlock).

Education, however, is *not* a fundamental right protected by the US Constitution. In fact, public education is not mentioned at all in the text of the Constitution. In the landmark case *San Antonio Independent School District v. Rodriguez* in 1973 (mentioned earlier),[11] the Supreme Court declined to invalidate a school funding scheme that resulted in per-pupil expenditures that varied widely from district to district based on differences in local property tax revenues. The 5–4 ruling explicitly held that education is *not* a fundamental right under the US Constitution and that therefore the funding scheme only had to pass a rational basis test. Which, of course, it did.

What's more, attendance zones "classify" children by residential address, putting them into different categories, and treating them differently, depending on whether they live inside or outside of the school attendance-zone boundary. Classifications based on where you live do *not* create a suspect class as defined by the court.

So the courts are very unlikely to apply strict scrutiny to attendance-zone boundaries, which would seem to imply that these policies are immune to constitutional challenge.

But there is another option.

Escape from the Framework

Let's step back for a minute. What exactly is the *equal protection of the law*? What does that phrase mean?

The Fourteenth Amendment was passed in the wake of the Civil War. Congress wanted to ensure that the states would not use laws to enforce racial prejudice or deny black Americans economic or political rights. But the relevant text of the amendment itself does not mention race at all. Section 1 states, in its entirety:

> All persons born or naturalized in the United States,
> and subject to the jurisdiction thereof, are citizens of
> the United States and of the State wherein they reside.
> No State shall make or enforce any law which shall
> abridge the privileges or immunities of citizens of the
> United States; nor shall any State deprive any person
> of life, liberty, or property, without due process of
> law; *nor deny to any person within its jurisdiction the equal
> protection of the laws.* [emphasis added]

The courts have generally held that this last clause—known as the Equal Protection Clause—means that individuals in a similar situation must be treated equally under the law. Equal Protection puts limits on the states, but the courts have ruled that it also applies to local governments, including school districts. And it also applies, via the legal concept of "reverse incorporation," to the federal government.

Presumably, the drafters of the Fourteenth Amendment were savvy enough to anticipate that outlawing racial discrimination was not enough. It was certainly possible—and perhaps inevitable—that politicians would find other means of reserving resources and rights for the politically powerful. And that's exactly what happened.

Royster Guano Company v. Virginia (1920)[12] was an early case that applied the Equal Protection Clause in a nonracial context. *Royster Guano* dealt with corporate income taxes, so I will spare you the case details, but here is the court's effort to define what equal protection means:

> It is unnecessary to say that the "equal protection of
> the laws" required by the Fourteenth Amendment
> does not prevent the States from resorting to classifi-
> cation for the purposes of legislation. Numerous and
> familiar decisions of this court establish that they have
> a wide range of discretion in that regard. *But the classi-*
> *fication must be reasonable, not arbitrary, and must rest upon*
> *some ground of difference having a fair and substantial rela-*
> *tion to the object of the legislation, so that all persons simi-*
> *larly circumstanced shall be treated alike.* [emphasis added]

And here's Chief Justice Warren Burger writing the court's opinion in the desegregation case *Reed v. Reed* (1971): "The Equal Protection Clause of [the Fourteenth] amendment does . . . deny to States the power to legislate that different treatment be accorded to persons placed by a statute into different classes on the basis of criteria wholly unrelated to the objective of that statute."[13]

Here is what I see as the strongest argument that attendance zones and geographic enrollment preferences violate the promise of equal protection:

1. The purpose of a state's education code is to establish a system of free public schools consistent with that state's constitution.

2. When a school district creates an attendance zone, the district places children into two classes (inside vs. outside) based on the criterion of that child's place of residence within the district.

3. When a child tries to enroll at a district school that is at capacity, she can be denied enrollment because she is classified as living outside the attendance zone.

4. A child's place of residence within the district is a criterion "wholly unrelated to the purpose" of the state's education laws. If two children live on opposite sides of the same street (but both within the jurisdictional boundaries of the school district), then these two children are "similarly circumstanced" relative to the purpose of the public education system.

5. Therefore, school attendance-zone boundaries and geographic enrollment preferences violate the Fourteenth Amendment's promise of "equal protection of the law." Any laws that allow or require school districts to establish these zones are therefore also unconstitutional.

An attendance zone is, in essence, a license for the school district to discriminate in its enrollment decisions. And on what basis is the district discriminating? Where you live. Not whether you live within the district's jurisdiction, but where you live *within the district.*

It's important to note once more that a school attendance-zone boundary has no legislative reality. Boundaries *between* school districts mark the borders between political subdivisions and are established through the democratic legislative process and carry the full weight of the law. Attendance zones, by contrast, are just lines drawn on a map by the staff of a governmental agency, the school district. As I discussed in Chapter Three, they are administrative entities.

Perhaps this wouldn't matter so much if all schools were approximately equal in quality—or at least in the same ballpark. But, as we saw in Chapter Two, schools in America vary greatly in quality, even within the same school district, even within the same neighborhood. These disparities exist within every large city in the country. An attendance-zone boundary is the classification method by which the best schools—those at capacity—let some kids in and keep others out.

How does this jibe with the court's distinction between strict scrutiny and rational basis review? Those standards of review are just tools, and sometimes tools fail. Not every tool works in every situation. In a handful of important cases over the last few decades, the court has invoked the Fourteenth Amendment to invalidate laws or state actions *even though strict scrutiny was not triggered.* In order to get around the limitations of the toothless rational basis standard, the court has created a third way under the banner of "intermediate scrutiny."

In these cases, the court has used different words to describe its standard of review. "Intermediate scrutiny" is one, but there is also "heightened scrutiny" and even "enhanced rational basis" scrutiny. As many scholars (and judges) have recognized, even the "enhanced rational basis" cases are really applying a type of intermediate scrutiny. For our purposes, we're going to say that all of these fall under the general umbrella of intermediate scrutiny.

It seems that the courts have created this intermediate form of scrutiny precisely because the standard framework will occasionally produce results that seem to be at odds with the courts' understanding of the essential meaning of the Equal Protection Clause. That is, cases considered under the rational basis test will sometimes produce results in which two classes of people are treated quite differently by state actors, even though the two classes are "similarly circumstanced" under the law. Intermediate scrutiny was created to relieve the court's discomfort with this outcome.

In order to beat the intermediate scrutiny test, the government must show that the law or policy in question advances "an important governmental objective" by means that are "substantially related" to that objective.[14] For example, intermediate scrutiny has been used by the courts to limit the following government activities:

- Gender restrictions on the purchase of alcohol—*Craig v. Boren* (1976)[15]
- Gender discrimination in the selection of juries—*J.E.B. v. Alabama* (1994)[16]
- Discrimination against people born out of wedlock—*Weber v. Aetna Casualty & Surety Company* (1972)[17]
- Discrimination against the mentally disabled—*City of Cleburne v. Cleburne Living Center* (1985)[18]
- Restrictions on content-neutral speech—*United States v. O'Brien* (1976)[19]
- Overly aggressive restrictions on the time, place, or manner of constitutionally protected speech—*Renton v. Playtime Theatres* (1986)[20]

I am particularly interested in two landmark cases in which the court applied intermediate scrutiny in the context of public education. In each case, state laws excluded a distinct class of people from enrolling in a particular institution of public education. Although education is not a "fundamental right" under the US Constitution, the courts have consistently ruled that it is indeed an "important government objective." A state law or policy that declares a certain set of people ineligible to enroll in a particular public school is a good candidate for a legal challenge under intermediate scrutiny.

Look at *United States v. Virginia* (1996).[21] In a 7–1 decision, the court
ruled that the State of Virginia could no longer restrict enrollment in the
Virginia Military Institute (VMI) to men. Virginia tried to set up an analogous school for women, the Virginia Women's Institute for Leadership
(VWIL), but the court ruled that the alternative school was not "substantially comparable" to VMI and that therefore the admissions policy "denies
equal protection to women." The court took issue with the "categorical
exclusion" of a specific class of potential students:

> Our precedent instructs that "benign" justifications
> proffered in defense of categorical exclusions will not
> be accepted automatically; a tenable justification must
> describe actual state purposes, not rationalizations for
> actions in fact differently grounded.

This is what a school attendance zone creates—a "categorical exclusion"
based on place of residence. And what about two neighboring schools—
one that is failing and one that is thriving? They cannot be said to be
"substantially comparable." In order to defend the existence of attendance
zones, the state or the school district would have to meet a high standard
of proof in relating those discriminatory policies to "actual state purposes."
If the court would be willing to apply intermediate scrutiny, I'm not sure
that the state or the school district would be able to clear that bar.

In a case from 1950 about segregated law schools, the court compared
the quality of the two available options:

> We cannot find substantial equality in the educational
> opportunities offered white and Negro law students
> by the State. In terms of number of the faculty, vari-
> ety of courses and opportunity for specialization, size
> of the student body, scope of the library, availability
> of law review and similar activities, the [whites-only]
> Law School is superior.... It is difficult to believe that

one who had a free choice between these law schools
would consider the question close.[22]

I believe that the court would similarly look askance at the discrepancies between a school like Lincoln Elementary in Chicago and its close
neighbor, Manierre Elementary. Would a family who had a "free choice"
between these schools consider them to be comparable or "substantially
equal"?

No, they wouldn't.

Next, let's look at *Plyler v. Doe* (1982),[23] another case in which the court
struck down a categorical exclusion that prevented a subset of people
from enrolling at a public education institution. I briefly discussed this
case at the outset of the chapter. The Texas legislature had passed a law
withholding from school districts all state educational funds designated for
students not "legally admitted" into the US and authorizing the districts
to deny enrollment to such children.

The court applied greater scrutiny to this law, using the following
rationale:

> We have recognized that certain forms of legislative
> classification, while not facially invidious, nonethe-
> less give rise to recurring constitutional difficulties; in
> these limited circumstances, we have sought the assur-
> ance that the classification reflects a reasoned judg-
> ment consistent with the ideal of equal protection by
> inquiring whether it may fairly be viewed as further-
> ing a substantial interest of the State.

The court held that such a law was not rationally related to any substantial goal of the state, especially given the potential harm to a discrete class
of "innocent children," as well as costs to the nation as a whole. And the
court specifically quoted the *Brown* decision in its reasoning:

What we said 28 years ago in *Brown v. Board of Education*, 347 US 483 (1954), still holds true: "Today, education is perhaps the most important function of state and local governments. Compulsory school attendance laws and the great expenditures for education both demonstrate our recognition of the importance of education to our democratic society. It is required in the performance of our most basic public responsibilities, even service in the armed forces. It is the very foundation of good citizenship. Today it is a principal instrument in awakening the child to cultural values, in preparing him for later professional training, and in helping him to adjust normally to his environment. In these days, it is doubtful that any child may reasonably be expected to succeed in life if he is denied the opportunity of an education. *Such an opportunity, where the state has undertaken to provide it, is a right which must be made available to all on equal terms.*" [emphasis added]

The great liberal justice Harry Blackmun, in a concurring opinion in *Plyler*, extends the logic of the "categorical exclusion" mentioned in *United States v. Virginia*: "In my view, when the State provides an education to some and denies it to others, it immediately and inevitably creates class distinctions of a type fundamentally inconsistent with those purposes . . . of the Equal Protection Clause."

The success of such a case could turn solely on whether the court would be convinced to apply intermediate scrutiny. Both *Plyler v. Doe* and *United States v. Virginia* provide compelling precedents that intermediate scrutiny is justified when one class of people is denied access to institutions of public education, because the court clearly believes that education is an important government objective.

Alternatively, intermediate scrutiny could also be triggered if the court decided that discrimination based on a child's residential address creates a quasi-suspect class. But this additional step would not be necessary to trigger intermediate scrutiny if the court were to apply the same reasoning about the importance of education as it did in *Plyler*.

As I discussed earlier, Justice Anthony Kennedy made it clear in 2007 that the Fourteenth Amendment cannot allow student assignment based on that student's race. From the majority opinion in *Parents Involved in Community Schools v. Seattle School District*:

> What the government is not permitted to do, absent a showing of necessity not made here, is to classify every student on the basis of race and to assign each of them to schools based on that classification.[24]

Imagine a ruling in which the court issued a similar statement about geographic discrimination:

> What the government is not permitted to do, absent a showing of necessity not made here, is to classify every student on the basis of their place of residence and to assign each of them to schools based on that classification.

Such a ruling would open up the best public schools to all district residents and could go a long way toward restoring faith in public education as a key component of the social compact.

Counterarguments

It will be no small task to convince the court to apply intermediate scrutiny. The court will have an easy out if it doesn't want to take on such a contentious issue: *Education isn't a fundamental right, and school attendance zones don't create a suspect class. We are therefore powerless to take a stand.*

But if the court is willing to consider these policies under the precedent of *Royster Guano Company* and other cases that first defined the essence of equal protection, then I think the court will be inclined to consider these policies with a skeptical eye.

As discussed in the last chapter, I am *not* suggesting that any child has the right to attend a specific school. But all the residents of a district deserve an *equal opportunity* to enroll in the best schools in the district. In a public-school lottery, for example, there are winners and losers. The results may seem frustrating or even tragic. But a lottery gives every district family a fair chance—an equal opportunity—to enroll their child at a coveted school that could dramatically change her life trajectory.

Of course, some will argue that the court already ruled that school districts can use residency requirements to determine eligibility for enroll-ment. That's what *Martinez v. Bynum* was about, right? But as we've discussed, *Martinez* only allows districts to conduct a residency check to confirm that the family lives within the legally defined jurisdictional boundaries of the entire school district. *Martinez* dealt with "*bona fide* residency tests," which governments are allowed to employ in order to determine who does or does not fall under their jurisdiction (e.g., for tax collection). *Martinez* does not address whether school-district officials can exclude a child from a given school solely based on where that child lives within the district. That is a very different legal question.

Some will argue that, even under intermediate scrutiny, school atten-dance zones are a way for the government to deliver on its promise of public education available for all citizens in a way that is "substantially related" to that purpose. Attendance zones provide local schools for all children.

But, as I discussed in Chapter Nine, this isn't quite right. In most states, students are not guaranteed a spot just because they live within that school's attendance-zone boundaries. And due to the irregular shapes of many attendance zones, students are often assigned to a school that is *not* the nearest to their home. If the legislature wants most kids to be able to go to school near their home, then there are many other options for achieving that goal, rather than relying on geography to determine enrollment eligibility. Access to other governmental services—such as health-care clinics or fire stations—is not conditioned on a residency test. So it's hard to see how these policies are necessary or even the most pragmatic option.

Other institutions of public education—for example, state university systems, community colleges, and child-care centers—do not require within-jurisdiction residency tests. As we've discussed, most public charter schools are already forbidden from restricting their enrollment to students in a specific geographic area of the district. Defenders of the status quo would be forced to argue that the government has a "compelling interest" in forbidding such discrimination by some public schools and requiring it for others.

I understand that the idea of challenging attendance zones on federal Equal Protection grounds can easily be dismissed, especially as the court has grown more rigid in recent decades in how it decides whether strict scrutiny or rational basis review applies. However, the early case law on Equal Protection is clear: The government cannot treat people vastly differently if those people are "similarly situated" under the law. This would strongly suggest that attendance-zone boundaries do not pass constitutional muster.

Getting rid of within-district residency tests for public-school children would go a long way toward finishing the job that *Brown* started sixty-six years ago—making public education available to all on equal terms.

Chapter 11
The School Closest to Your Residence?

The courts aren't the only players in the civil rights game, and the Fourteenth Amendment is not the only relevant law. In the 1960s and 1970s, Congress stepped in to pass critical legislation that would provide even more protection for Americans' civil rights, and especially those of racial minorities, in key areas of public life.

Some of the most historic legislation of the last century emerged in this area of the law. The Civil Rights Acts of 1957 and 1964, as well as the Voting Rights Act of 1965, put even more restrictions on state actions meant to discriminate against racial minorities and empowered the Department of Justice to intervene when civil rights were violated.

Redlining and other discriminatory practices in the housing and mortgage markets were outlawed, not by the federal courts, but by congressional action via the Fair Housing Act of 1968 and the Community Reinvestment Act of 1977.

Congress has also weighed in on civil rights and equal access in our public schools. In 1974, the Democratic Congress passed the Equal Educational Opportunities Act (EEOA).[1] It was signed into law on August 21 by Republican president Gerald Ford. This little-known federal law governs how states and districts assign children to public schools. It aims to restrict practices that encourage and exacerbate the racial divisions in our education system.

Somehow this law has escaped much public scrutiny. It's actually quite powerful. And it may invalidate the boundary lines of every single attendance zone in the country.Yes, that's right. It appears that the shape of every attendance zone in America is in violation of federal civil rights law.

One of the Most Difficult Issues of Our Time

Kamala Harris and Joe Biden are not the first elected officials to be caught in a political bind by the issue of desegregation and federally mandated busing of schoolchildren.

In March 1972, President Nixon was feeling boxed in by the same issue. Many federal courts were signing off on busing plans that would force the integration of public schools in districts that had previously engaged in overt segregation. But members of both parties—including Joe Biden[2]—were urging the passage of a constitutional amendment that would forbid the courts from ordering busing.

Nixon was opposed to busing for the purposes of desegregation, but also wanted to express sympathy for children caught in failing schools that were divided along racial lines. So, on March 17, he delivered an address to the American people, offering a compromise. He offered his commitment to the idea of providing "a better education for every child in America in a desegregated school system."[3] He proposed a moratorium on federally mandated busing but also a "companion measure" called the Equal Educational Opportunities Act, which would increase funding for the inner-city schools, especially those attended by ethnic minorities.

That law, the EEOA, wouldn't be signed for another two years. And Nixon would have to negotiate with lawmakers in order to get it through Congress. The resulting law is a strange mix of high-minded goals and status-quo-ism. It's all there in the first sentence of the law:

> The Congress declares it to be the policy of the
> United States that—(1) all children enrolled in public
> schools are entitled to equal educational opportunity
> without regard to race, color, sex, or national origin;
> and (2) the neighborhood is the appropriate basis for

determining public school assignments.[4]

On the one hand, it promises equal opportunity. On the other hand, it provides legal cover for neighborhood-based schools and district-drawn attendance zones. By 1974, the government had already played a major role in segregating American neighborhoods, so a system based on neighborhood schools would, by default, create schools divided along racial lines. The EEOA also implicitly endorses the *assignment* of students to schools by the district or the state.

But Mephistopheles is in the minutiae, as they say. Here's what the EEOA has to say about the assignment of minority children to public schools:

> No State shall deny equal educational opportunity to an individual on account of his or her race, color, sex, or national origin, by ... the assignment by an educational agency of a student to a school, other than the one closest to his or her place of residence within the school district in which he or she resides, if the assignment results in a greater degree of segregation of students on the basis of race, color, sex, or national origin among the schools of such agency than would result if such student were assigned to the school closest to his or her place of residence within the school district of such agency providing the appropriate grade level and type of education for such student.

This is *incredible*. For minority children, federal law defines the neighborhood school as "the one closest to his or her place of residence within the school district in which he or she resides." And Congress prohibits the district from assigning a minority child to another school, if it will result in "a greater degree of segregation."

I don't think the full implications of that language have been understood.

As I discussed in Chapter Two, most attendance zones are irregular in shape. Some zones seem to display a pattern of gerrymandering in which white students are disproportionately assigned to one set of schools, and minorities are disproportionately assigned to others.

There is surprisingly little case law relevant to the EEOA. The major cases all deal with other provisions of the law, such as its requirement that states and districts take "appropriate action" to overcome obstacles to education that arise from language barriers.[5] I've been unable to find any case law that interprets and applies the clause of the EEOA that governs student assignment.

Figure 11.1 shows the attendance zone for Mount Washington Elementary in Los Angeles and all of the surrounding elementary schools. For families who live in the shaded areas, Mount Washington is their closest school. But the children living in those areas are assigned to other schools that are farther away. Because Mount Washington is so much "whiter" than the surrounding schools, LA Unified is creating a "greater degree of segregation" by sending minority students living in those areas to other, more distant schools.

The Los Angeles Unified School District is clearly in violation of the EEOA by assigning those minority children to other schools. Any minority student living in those areas—black, Hispanic, Asian, Native American— would be able to file a claim in the federal courts, asking the courts to force Mount Washington Elementary to allow them to enroll or—at the very least—to offer them an equal opportunity to enroll. Similar maps could be created for every one of the elite public schools that I discuss in Chapter Two and Appendix A, as well as many others across the country.

What's even more interesting is how the EEOA might interact with

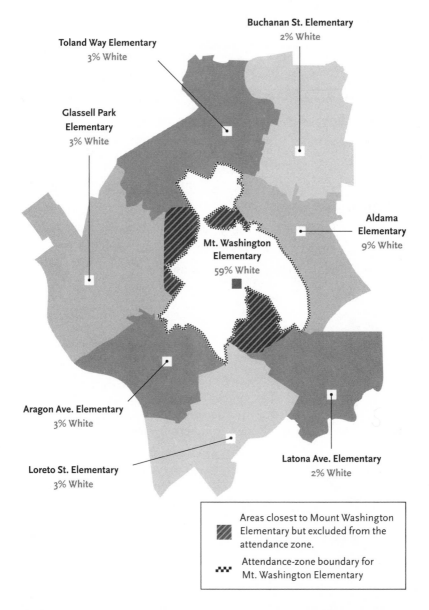

Buchanan St. Elementary
2% White

Toland Way Elementary
3% White

Glassell Park Elementary
3% White

Aldama Elementary
9% White

Mt. Washington Elementary
59% White

Aragon Ave. Elementary
3% White

Loreto St. Elementary
3% White

Latona Ave. Elementary
2% White

Areas closest to Mount Washington Elementary but excluded from the attendance zone.

Attendance-zone boundary for Mt. Washington Elementary

Figure 11.1 Like most attendance zones, Mount Washington Elementary in Los Angeles violates a federal civil rights law that prohibits minority students from being assigned to a school that is not the nearest to their home if it exacerbates segregation.

Source: Los Angeles Unified School District, California Department of Education

recent court rulings, such as *Parents Involved in Community Schools [PICS] v. Seattle School District*, which forbid school officials from using a student's race to determine where the student will go to school. If the district is forbidden from assigning a minority student to a school that is not the nearest to his or her home, the logic of the *PICS* ruling would suggest that the district is also then forbidden from sending a white student to a school that is not nearest his or her home, because race cannot be the determining factor in school assignment.

Under such constraints, the only legal attendance zone is one that sends every single student to the school nearest his or her home. Attendance zones, as currently drawn, would be invalid.

Chapter 12
Equal Racial Access to Schools?

"I grew up seeing how the zip code one is born in determines much of their opportunity."[1]

That's a 2018 tweet from Alexandria Ocasio-Cortez, the Democratic congresswoman from New York and champion of social justice. The tweet got over 80,000 retweets and likes. She's acknowledging something we all know about American society.

Why is your zip code so influential in determining your fate? It's complicated, of course, and there are probably many answers. But if you had to point to one single factor, it would almost certainly be this: Where you live determines the public schools in which you're allowed to enroll.

There are huge disparities in the quality of public schools, even those just blocks away from one another. State laws and school-district policies assign some children to the best schools, leaving others on the outside, based on residential address.

If we're looking to give everyone a fair shot at the American Dream, that can't be the best way to do it.

Still Unequal, Still Separate

Did *Brown v. Board of Education* succeed or fail?

In one way, it was clearly a success. In 1951, little Linda Brown was denied enrollment at Sumner Elementary because of her race. Because of the *Brown* ruling, that can't happen to a child now (at least not legally). School districts no longer have explicit policies that restrict school enrollment based on a student's race, and *Brown* is rightly recognized as a landmark achievement even by many Americans who don't follow politics, education policy, or legal history.

Of course it is now conventional wisdom that *Brown* has also failed. At the highest level, the court wanted to end racial inequality in the schools. Writing for the unanimous Supreme Court, Chief Justice Earl Warren held that "separate educational facilities are inherently unequal," and thus "separate" systems are disallowed. But sixty-six years later, our schools remain divided along racial lines and starkly unequal in performance.

There's one more way that *Brown* has been a failure. Here's the pertinent quote from Warren's opinion:

> In these days, it is doubtful that any child may
> reasonably be expected to succeed in life if he is
> denied the opportunity of an education. Such an
> opportunity, where the state has undertaken to
> provide it, is a right which must be made available to
> all on equal terms.[2]

Justice Warren found that enrollment in Sumner Elementary in 1951 Topeka was not "available to all on equal terms." Almost seven decades later, Lincoln Elementary in Chicago is still not "available to all on equal terms." Nor is Ivanhoe Elementary in Los Angeles, Mary Lin Elementary in Atlanta, John Hay Elementary in Seattle, Penn Alexander School in Philadelphia, or Lakewood Elementary in Dallas.

In 1951, they used Linda Brown's race to keep her out of Sumner. In 2020, they use a line drawn down the middle of North Avenue to keep Old Town kids out of Lincoln Elementary.

The writer Malcolm Gladwell has argued that the courts got something important wrong in the desegregation cases that followed *Brown*. They forced black children into formerly all-white schools. In the process, many black children were taken out of perfectly good schools and bused to all-white schools, and the black teachers at the black school often lost their jobs.

Gladwell argues, persuasively, that desegregation cases should have been about *access*. That's what Linda Brown's parents were asking for. They didn't even want to move their precious little girl to a different school. They just didn't want her to be automatically excluded from a perfectly good public school on the basis of her race. Here's her mother, Leola, speaking to an interviewer from the Kansas State Historical Society.

> *Interviewer:* You didn't want your daughter to go to the white school because the white school was better than the black school?
>
> *Leola Brown:* Oh, no. That never came up. We were getting a quality education at Monroe [the black school].[3]

The Browns simply wanted fair access to the public school that they thought was right for their daughter.

Racially Equal Schools vs. Equal Racial Access to Schools

At least one Supreme Court justice saw the wisdom in focusing on equal access.

Writing in 1992, Justice Antonin Scalia argued that we should open up the public schools to all comers. He imagined an educational system "in which parents are free to disregard neighborhood-school assignment, and to send their children (with transportation paid) to whichever school they choose."[4]

Justice Scalia was writing a concurring opinion in the *Freeman v. Pitts* desegregation case, which considered when a school district could be declared free of court supervision after eliminating the effects of explicit segregation. Scalia agreed with the majority opinion, but disagreed (as he often did) with their muddled reasoning. The context is important, because the case law around desegregation is so muddy and counterintuitive. Justice Scalia was pointing a way out of the morass.

And what a morass.

As we've discussed, it's illegal for a district to intentionally segregate its students by race. The courts have ruled that, once *de jure* or intentional segregation has been found in some of a district's schools, then it can be assumed that other segregated schools in the district are operating unlawfully. However, the converse is also true: If intentional segregation cannot be proven, then even schools that display the most egregious forms of racial separation are allowed by the law.

Once the courts find that a district has intentionally used policy to segregate its schools by race, then the district must make changes that bring the district into "unitary" status. That's an unhelpful term meant to convey that all vestiges of prior intentional segmentation have been eliminated; thus the district is "unitary" and not divided.

When districts were found guilty of intentional segregation, two of the most common ways for them to try to decrease the racial divisions in their schools were (1) the creation of magnet schools to lure wealthier white students to inner-city campuses, and (2) busing students out of their neighborhood. Busing students was specifically validated by the courts as a way to prevent residential segregation from perpetuating racial divisions in the schools that were originally established through intentionally segregationist policies.[5]

Once the district is judged to be unitary, the district can immediately end all its efforts to desegregate. At that point, if the separation of the races reoccurs due to persistent residential segregation, then the resulting schools, now *de facto* segregated rather than *de jure*, are immune to legal challenge.[6]

Now we see how and why the court's rulings on desegregation, both complex and counterintuitive, have been both successful and unsuccessful.

Even in the nation's most racially divided cities, there are no longer any school districts that operate with an open intent to segregate the races in separate schools. And why would there be? All the district has to do is strike the mention of race from its student assignment policies, and the courts no longer have the ability to intervene. Problem solved.

As a result of this easy way out, segregation lawsuits against public school districts have all but disappeared. Nowadays, it is much more likely that the courts will rule that a *desegregation* plan is unconstitutional, because it uses a child's race to determine which school the child will be assigned to. See *Parents Involved in Community Schools v. Seattle School District*, discussed in Chapter Ten.

Justice Scalia foresaw that districts would adapt to the law and that segregation lawsuits would be increasingly difficult to win. Contrary to what his liberal critics may have expected, he did not see this as a favorable outcome:

> If, as is normally the case under our equal protec-
> tion jurisprudence (and in the law generally), we
> require the plaintiffs to establish the asserted facts
> entitling them to relief—that the racial imbalance
> they wish corrected is at least in part the vestige of an
> old *de jure* system—the plaintiffs will almost always
> lose. Conversely, if we alter our normal approach and
> require the school authorities to establish the nega-
> tive—that the imbalance is not attributable to their
> past discrimination—the plaintiffs will almost always
> win....
>
> Since neither of these alternatives is entirely palatable,
> an observer unfamiliar with the history surrounding
> this issue might suggest that we avoid the problem by
> requiring only that the school authorities establish

a regime in which parents are free to disregard
neighborhood-school assignment, and to send their
children (with transportation paid) to whichever
school they choose. So long as there is free choice,
he would say, there is no reason to require that the
schools be made identical. The constitutional right
is equal racial access to schools, not access to racially
equal schools.

Justice Scalia predicted not only the demise of segregation lawsuits against school districts but also that the court's approach to *de jure* segregation would, in the long run, leave the courts powerless to address any imbalances that emerged as a result of neighborhood school assignment. He saw that "neighborhood-school assignment" would exclude most American kids from enrolling in the best public schools.

Scalia was right.

The Unfinished Project That Started Sixty-Six Years Ago

I've come to believe that we have left undone the primary work of the civil rights movement as it relates to the public schools. We abandoned the project that started with *Brown*. We did not open up our public schools to all comers, not even all those children within the same school district.

We have the chance to do that now, through either legislation or litigation. Doing so won't result in fully integrated schools. It won't mean that suddenly all schools will perform equally well. It won't solve all of the difficult problems that our public schools face.

But it will open up all kinds of opportunities for children who are currently stuck. School attendance zones have been tremendously destructive to the social compact. Poor families know that there are good or even great public schools in their district, maybe even just down the road. But their children aren't allowed to attend those schools. Who is allowed to attend? Wealthier people who pay through their mortgage or their rent for access to these public schools that are "public" in name only.

All families deserve to know that their children have an equal opportunity to attend the best public schools—and equal access to the rewards of attending such schools. We can—and should—offer that opportunity.

It's the right thing to do.

AFTERWORD
by Gloria Romero

_____

Education is the key to the American Dream. We all know it.

But what if, after all this time, we discover that the schoolhouse door is locked and that the keys issued to working-class families don't fit the lock, leaving millions of children—many of them poor black and Latino—on the outside of the American Dream looking in?

What then?

And what if, upon further inspection, we learn—despite all the inspirational phrases in our state constitutions and the court decisions holding education to be a fundamental right—that it is *state laws* that keep the schoolhouse doors closed?

This is the power of Tim DeRoche's *A Fine Line*, a no-holds-barred examination of the state laws and district policies that keep our schools separate and unequal.

Years have passed since Tim and I first sat down to ruminate about education inequity. During our first meeting, I shared with him my history of serving in the California Senate and my role in both education and prison reform. During those years, I dug deep into the school-to-prison pipeline and tried to hold California accountable for its shabby academic outcomes—particularly for children of color. As a senator, I received all the bureaucratic reports about California's hundreds of "chronically academically underperforming" schools. Year after year, nothing changed.

Angered by what I saw, I started writing bills to identify and turn around (or shut down) those continually failing schools. The bureaucrats railed against me. Despite the fact that I was a union member, the unions assailed me, condemning me for "shaming" these failing schools by publicly naming them. They objected to my efforts to give more options to the parents of kids trapped in these failure factories.

The vast majority of my fellow Democratic colleagues began to divorce themselves from any association with me, voting against bills that tried to empower parents and end the hegemony of zip code in the California schools. By refusing to stand up to union pressure, my colleagues were condemning many kids to the fast track into California's also failed correctional system. In my final election, status quo interests led by these unions, purporting to stand for "working families," spent an estimated $4 million to "kill the messenger." It didn't work.

What has changed since Tim and I first met?

California's public schools are more segregated today than ever. Advances have been made in establishing independent charter schools, which at the very least provide additional options for kids assigned to failing neighborhood schools. But California's academic outcomes have barely improved at most public schools, and year after year this is explained away by school officials. Consultants continue to get healthy gigs to fix what's wrong, but nothing much changes. As of this writing, only half of all California students perform at grade level in reading, which is an indictment of the *schools*, not the kids. An even higher number—about 60%—are underwater in math. In eleventh grade, the only grade tested in high school, barely one-fifth of low-income students are at grade level, compared to about half of their more affluent peers. And our schools have made zero progress in closing the performance gap facing the state's African American students, with only one in five performing at grade level in math. It bears repeating: This is a failure of the schools, not the children.

Many may be surprised to learn that education is *not* a fundamental right protected by the US Constitution. In fact, public education is not mentioned at all in the text of the Constitution. It is the state constitutions where education is hailed as an important responsibility of the government, and even a right. Despite the noble words enshrined in these state constitutions, state laws and school-district practices maintain a system of "educational redlining" in which school-district attendance zones permit only a chosen few to gain access to schools of excellence.

As I write this, our national media have been stoking outrage—and racking up ratings—covering the college admissions cheating and bribery scandal. Operation Varsity Blues, as it was called by the FBI, shined a glaring light on the power of money and privilege in ensuring that families with means can enter our nation's finest halls of knowledge through side doors that the rest of us can't access.

Yet the national media have been unwilling to look at the equally outrageous policies that keep working-class families out of the best public elementary schools. No one is paying attention to the scandalous system that determines a five-year-old's educational destiny based on his or her address. If education is the key to the American Dream, millions of children are being issued defective keys.

Also as I write this, our nation is embroiled in an increasingly contentious presidential campaign, and the Democratic candidates loudly bemoan the inequalities of our society, vowing to break up corporate monopolies. Yet these same candidates refuse to mention the single largest monopoly and the primary cause of educational inequality in our country—the laws and policies that assign children to different public schools based on where they live.

Virtually every Democratic candidate is chasing coveted dollars from the national teachers' unions, which are powerful power brokers in Washington and the state capitols. These unions fight to maintain the current system that keeps so many working-class children, of all races and income levels, from enrolling in the best public schools.

You could argue that the current system is a feudalistic land model whereby children, starting in kindergarten, are assigned to attend "neighborhood schools" on the basis of their home address. The system relies on school-district bureaucrats who draw up arbitrary "attendance zones" that snake through our neighborhoods, giving students on one side of the street the opportunity to enroll in an elite public school, while denying entrance to those on the other side of the street.

To make matters worse, more affluent families move into the zone with the good school, inflating local property values and boxing out even more families. On the other side of the line, property values languish. Just ask any realtor what the power of a "good school district" or "the right zone" means in terms of the price of a typical home.

Attendance zones and geographic enrollment preferences are a blatant, if unacknowledged, echo of the shameful practice of redlining, which denied black and Latino neighborhoods access to mortgages and federal housing assistance. Just as redlining in the real estate market was forbidden by federal civil rights law, so too should "educational redlining" be made illegal.

I still consider myself an optimist, and I believe that these laws and policies will eventually end up in the dustbin of history where they belong. My mother only attended school through the sixth grade. But she understood the value of education and ensured that all six of her children graduated from high school. Some of us, including me, earned a college degree. After being elected to the state Senate, I became chair of its Education Committee.

After leaving the Senate, I went on to become the cofounder of the independent public charter school Scholarship Prep, which has defied the odds and demonstrated that high-poverty children—when given an escape hatch from their assigned school—can excel and get on a track for success in college and beyond.

By that time my mom had passed away, but I never forgot her powerful desire for educational opportunities for her kids. I thought of her when I met with the constituents I represented in East Los Angeles, and I think of her today when I meet the families we serve at Scholarship Prep. Those kids resemble me as a child; those mothers resemble my mother. As long as I'm alive, I will continue to fight for their right to have a fair shot at the American Dream.

Because of what my mom taught me, I admire any parents who are willing to do what they need to do to secure educational opportunities for their children. No one should be denied those opportunities because of where they live.

We all know that more affluent families go shopping for their schools— usually by buying a home in the neighborhood of their choice. Many working-class parents seek out other options too, as they should if they are assigned to a failing school (or, for that matter, a good school that isn't a fit for their child). That's why it's so important to support high-performing, free, public charter schools that are open to any resident of the school district, no matter where she lives. Charter schools defy zip code and give working-class families an escape hatch, even if those families are unjustly denied a fair right to enroll in a high-performing traditional public school just down the street.

One lesson we can take from the college cheating scandal is that motivated parents will seek out the best option for their child. Like other parent advocates around the country, I was outraged to see those wealthy parents get off with a slap on the wrist. Working-class parents accused of "educational fraud" in the public K–12 system have often faced much harsher penalties just for trying to get their children out of failing public schools.

Kelley Williams-Bolar, the single African American mother from Akron, Ohio, is for me the Rosa Parks of the parent empowerment movement. When her family was assigned to a failing, unsafe school, she refused to comply and instead used a family member's address to get her kids into a safer school district nearby. District officials wanted to make an example of Williams-Bolar for the crime of "stealing an education," and charged her with two felonies. She had no money or connections to quietly bribe her way through a side door.

Tanya McDowell faced similar charges in Norwalk, Connecticut, for "stealing an education." Going after this single homeless mother, district officials brought criminal charges that carried *up to twenty years* in prison. School officials acknowledged that they treated McDowell more harshly than others because, as with Williams-Bolar, they wanted to make an example of her. Ironically, Norwalk school officials seemed committed to ensuring that a homeless family be bound by their "address."

In the aftermath of prosecution, these parents have banded together to protest the unfairness of our education policies. With Ms. Bolar, I flew across the country to a courthouse in Montgomery County, Pennsylvania, to support Hamlet Garcia, another parent charged with "stealing" a public education.

When Hamlet and Olesia Garcia separated, Olesia and their five-year-old daughter moved in with Olesia's father in adjacent, more affluent Montgomery County. But the little girl's darker skin tone "stuck out" in that largely white suburban neighborhood. Not long afterward—like Kelley Williams-Bolar and Tanya McDowell—Hamlet, Olesia, and her father were arrested, all accused of fraud for claiming a false address for their child.

If convicted, the Garcias could have served *up to seven years in prison.* Without the resources to engage in an extended legal battle, Mr. Garcia agreed to plead guilty to a misdemeanor offense, enabling his wife and father-in-law to be spared. Supported by the National Parents Union and the New York City Parents Union, Hamlet subsequently launched a courageous crusade to end these types of laws in the US.

After leaving the state Senate, I continued to vociferously advocate for breaking zip code–based educational policies in order to give poor black and Latino children equal access to the American Dream. You may be surprised by who was opposed to such commonsense reforms to benefit poor, minority children. The chair of the Los Angeles County Democratic Party at the time issued a directive to me and Democrats for Education Reform, for whom I was working, that we "cease and desist" from calling ourselves Democrats. As a proud lifelong Democrat, I was unwilling to succumb to the arrogance of his order.

Once, it was the Democratic Party that took the lead on these civil rights issues. Democratic leaders sponsored and passed important civil rights laws, such as the Civil Rights Acts of 1964, the Voting Rights Act of 1965, and the Fair Housing Act of 1968. We betray the legacy of those Democrats who came before us when we side with powerful interest groups rather than with working-class families and children of color.

Back in the 1970s, President Nixon wanted to pass a law that would make it harder to desegregate the schools. Democrats pushed back and forged a key compromise that made it illegal for minority children to be assigned to a school other than the one "closest to their residence" if doing so would exacerbate segregation. That law became the Equal Educational Opportunities Act of 1974.

As Tim points out in Chapter Eleven, every irregularly shaped attendance zone in America appears to violate this law. Now, decades later, we realize that this law could be a key part of a legal strategy to open up the elite public schools to more working-class families.

Of course, it would be much better if Congress or the state legislatures took immediate legislative action to end this kind of discrimination. One potential law would forbid school-district officials from excluding a child from a particular school because of the child's address within the district. Another potential law would open up every public school to a child who lives within any school district in the state. This is exactly what the California legislature did back in the 1980s when it stopped assigning Californians to community colleges based on their residential address. If this works for higher education, why can't it work for k–12 schools? Fair access to high-quality schools should be a universal right.

But I fear that politicians in both parties will not show the resolve necessary to stand up to special interests and open up the best public schools to the public. Tim argues, and I concur, that it is time to ask the courts to weigh in on attendance zones and geographic enrollment preferences. These laws and policies appear to violate constitutional protections provided by many states, including some that promise public schools "open to all" and others that promise "equality of educational opportunity."

Tim even argues persuasively that some of these laws and policies violate the court's original interpretation of the Fourteenth Amendment's promise of "the equal protection of the law." The courts have generally held that the Equal Protection Clause means that individuals in a similar situation must be treated equally under the law. District officials appear to violate this promise when they sort children into elite or failing public schools based solely on whether they live on one side of the street or the other.

Sixty-six years after *Brown v. Board of Education*, it is no longer enough to simply pay homage to another anniversary of this landmark decision. It is time to identify a twenty-first-century Linda Brown—and a Diego?—to walk down to the elite public school in the neighborhood and knock on the door. When the kids are refused entrance because they live on the wrong side of a line, it will be time to dispatch the lawyers to the federal courthouse once again.

Now that you've finished Tim's book, take a close look at your own state constitution. What does it say about education? It's time to bring state laws and district policies into alignment with the original promise of the public schools. Too many children have been separated from the American Dream, and now we need to invoke the courage of Thurgood Marshall and the Browns. It's time to give all American kids a key to the door that opens up the American Dream.

Sen. [Ret.] Gloria Romero
Fall 2019

APPENDIX A

TWO SIDES OF THE STREET

Below is a sample of neighboring schools within the same school district that share an attendance-zone boundary, yet show dramatically different patterns of performance and demographics. If you know of other such pairs, let us know on Twitter (@timderoche).

ATLANTA: Mary Lin Elem. vs. Hope-Hill Elem.

In 2012, Atlanta Public Schools proposed adjusting the school-assignment boundaries in the northeast sector to cope with overcrowding at sought-after schools as young families moved back to urban neighborhoods. The proposed changes would have cut the size of the attendance zone feeding into overcrowded—and coveted—Mary Lin Elementary, where a third of the students took classes in trailers.[1] In addition, some of those kids would have been assigned to under-enrolled Hope-Hill Elementary, two-and-a-half miles away in the Old Fourth Ward neighborhood, once home to Dr. Martin Luther King Jr.

Outraged parents filled district meetings to protest the proposals. "Mary Lin parents will pull their kids out of the lower-performing school," said one parent of a potential Mary Lin student.[2] The Mary Lin parents ultimately prevailed in their effort to preserve the existing attendance zone and secured an additional $18 million in funding to expand the school.[3] The wealthy Inman Park area remained within the attendance boundaries that fed into overcrowded Mary Lin, even though most Inman Park homes are actually located closer to Hope-Hill.

"You have to live within the school zone" to get into the school, says a staff member who answers the general office line. "It's kind of tricky. Some people have bought houses, and they thought they were zoned for us. But they weren't."[4]

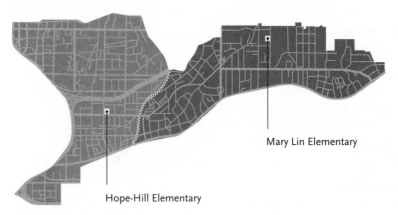

Mary Lin Elementary

Hope-Hill Elementary

Percentage of Students

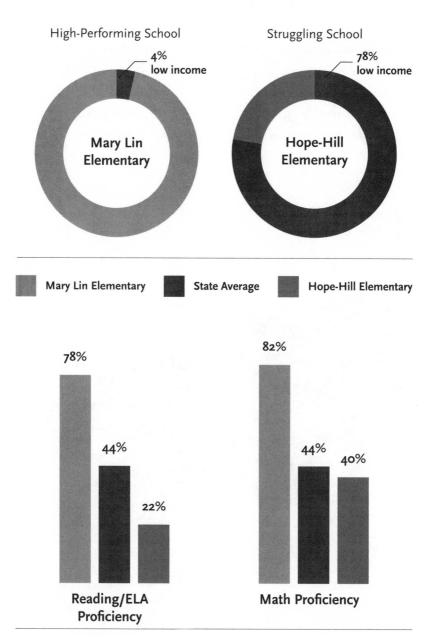

Source: Atlanta Public Schools, 2018–19

COLUMBUS: Clinton Elem. vs. Como Elem.

Clinton Elementary and Como Elementary serve the neighborhoods north and east of nearby Ohio State University in Columbus, Ohio. You can apply for a lottery to get into high-performing Clinton Elementary, even if you don't live in the geographic attendance zone. But, according to a staffer at the School Choice Division of Columbus City Schools, lottery spots are a "long shot" for students hoping to get into schools like Clinton, because so many families move inside the attendance zone in order to gain access.[5]

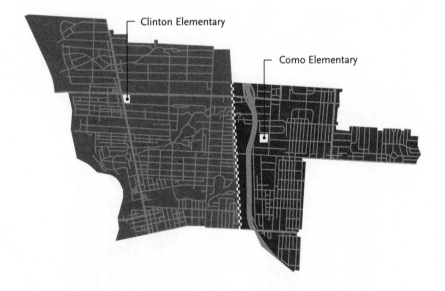

Clinton Elementary

Como Elementary

Percentage of Students

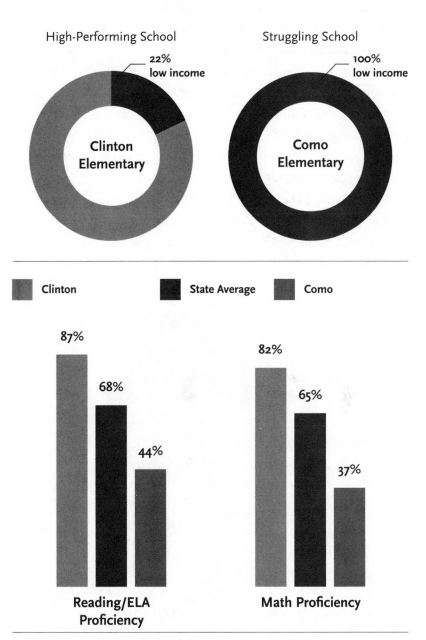

Source: Ohio Department of Education, 2017–18

DALLAS: Lakewood Elem. vs. Mount Auburn Elem.

In 2014, the Dallas Independent School District approved a $12.6 million addition to Lakewood Elementary School, despite plenty of room at nearby elementary schools Eduardo Mata and Mount Auburn. Mata, for example, was operating at only 35% of its enrollment capacity, with over four hundred seats available for students,[6] and was within walking distance of home for many Lakewood students. But the district caved to the wealthy political forces opposed to altering the boundaries of the attendance maps. "When you're talking about redrawing the boundaries of a Blue Ribbon school, the resistance is going to be very, very high," said district trustee Dan Micciche. As a result, Dallas taxpayers paid $12.6 million to build additional classroom seats at Lakewood Elementary—when there were plenty of available seats at a public school just down the road.[7]

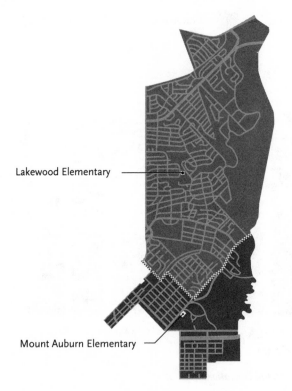

Lakewood Elementary

Mount Auburn Elementary

Percentage of Students

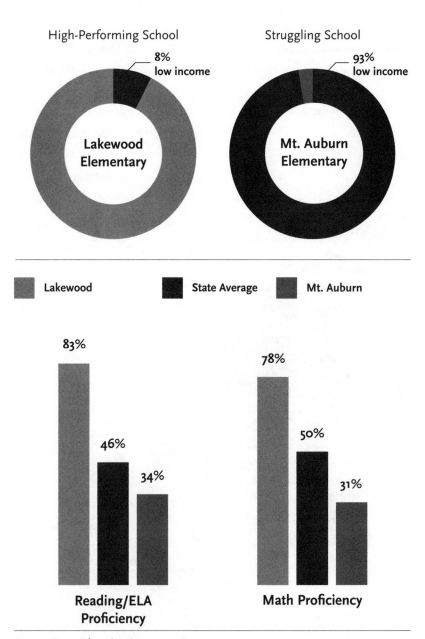

Source: *Texas Education Agency, 2018–19*

DENVER: Cory Elem. vs. Ellis Elem.

Denver has a school choice program in which parents are allowed to list school preferences for their kids, and the district tries to allot spaces to families based on those preferences.[8] But that doesn't mean that Denver has scrapped attendance zones and the geographic enrollment preferences that keep kids out of some of the best public schools. At popular Cory Elementary in the Cory-Merrill neighborhood, a staffer reports that the school admits only 10%–15% of the students who apply from outside Cory's attendance zone. That would include any applicants from nearby Ellis Elementary, which has much poorer student performance. "If you want a guarantee," says the Cory staffer, "move into the boundaries."[9]

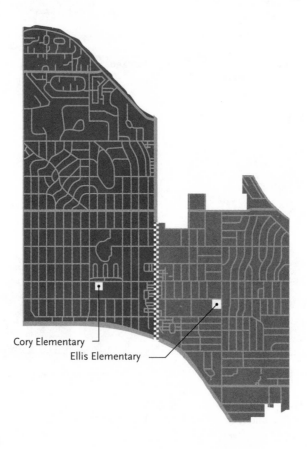

Cory Elementary
Ellis Elementary

Percentage of Students

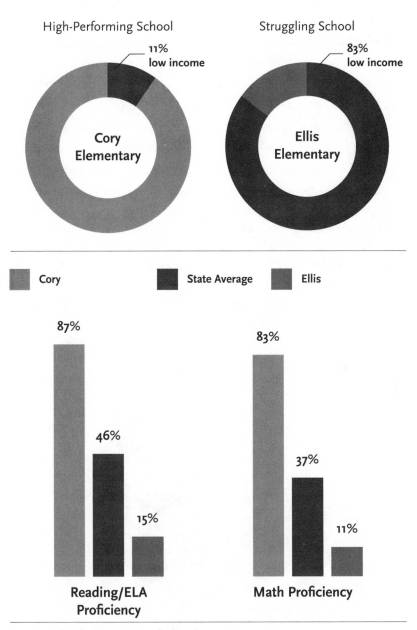

Source: Colorado Department of Education, 2018–19

FORT LAUDERDALE: Bayview Elem. vs. Bennett Elem.

In Fort Lauderdale, Bayview Elementary School shares an attendance-zone boundary more than two miles long with Bennett Elementary School. The two schools are just 1,000 feet from each other but couldn't be further apart in terms of performance and demographics.

Broward County Public Schools offers a "tool" for you to find your school: "You must provide your specific street address and your child's grade level, and the office will determine the correct school your child is supposed to attend."[10] I wonder how many families assigned to Bennett consider that struggling school to be "the correct school" for their children.

The policy is almost comically draconian, including the gratuitous use of ALL CAPS: "STUDENTS ARE TO ATTEND THE SCHOOL TO WHICH THEY ARE BOUNDARIED, ON THE BASIS OF THE GEOGRAPHICAL BOUNDARY IN WHICH THE PARENT(S) RESIDE... IN ORDER TO ENSURE THAT STUDENTS ARE ENROLLED IN THEIR ASSIGNED SCHOOL, PARENTS MUST PROVIDE VALID DOCUMENTATION AT THE START OF THE SCHOOL YEAR ON THE DAY OF ENROLLMENT DURING THE SCHOOL YEAR. SCHOOL PERSONNEL WILL APPLY STRATEGIES AVAILABLE, IN A TIMELY MANNER, TO VERIFY DOCUMENTATION PROVIDED."[11]

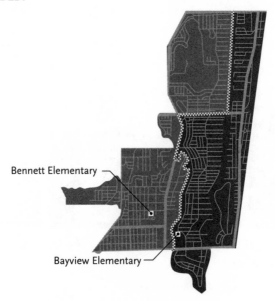

Bennett Elementary

Bayview Elementary

Percentage of Students

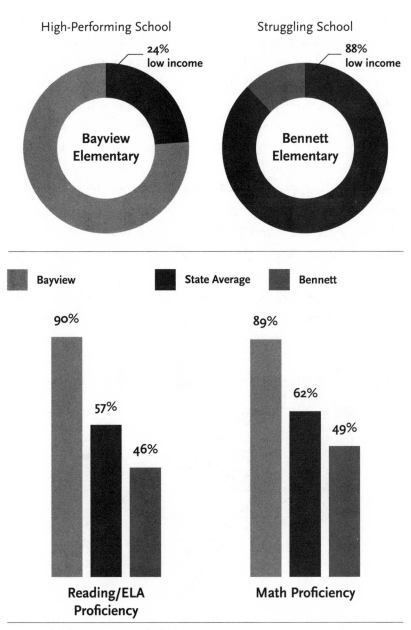

High-Performing School

24%
low income

Bayview
Elementary

Struggling School

88%
low income

Bennett
Elementary

Bayview   State Average   Bennett

90%

57%

46%

Reading/ELA
Proficiency

89%

62%

49%

Math Proficiency

Source: Florida Department of Education, 2018–19

INDIANAPOLIS:
Center for Inquiry 84 vs. Butler University Lab School 55

Indianapolis uses "proximity maps" to determine preferred enrollment for its most sought-after schools. The *Indianapolis Star* says this about the school they call Center for Inquiry 84: "It boasts an intensely rigorous curriculum. Experienced teachers. National awards for excellence."[12]

A few years ago, the proximity map gave an enrollment preference for kids who lived in an approximate one-mile radius from the school. But the school ended up with a waiting list of over five hundred because of families flooding into that desirable circle on the map. "So they tightened it up to a half-mile," says a school staffer. But even with the more tightly drawn zone, there's no guarantee you'll get in: "It's never been like you for sure are in if you're within a half a mile," she says, "because, unfortunately, oftentimes, depending on the year, we have more families within that half mile than we have seats in our school."[13]

Brian Fife was chair of the Department of Public Policy at a local university in Fort Wayne. "It seems that some folks are being left out, and that is disconcerting and problematic," Fife told the *Star*.

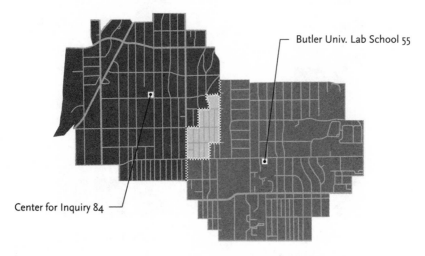

Note: Kids in the light-shaded area between the two schools have a "proximity preference" for both schools, but such a preference only matters for the school that is full, CFI 84.

Percentage of Students

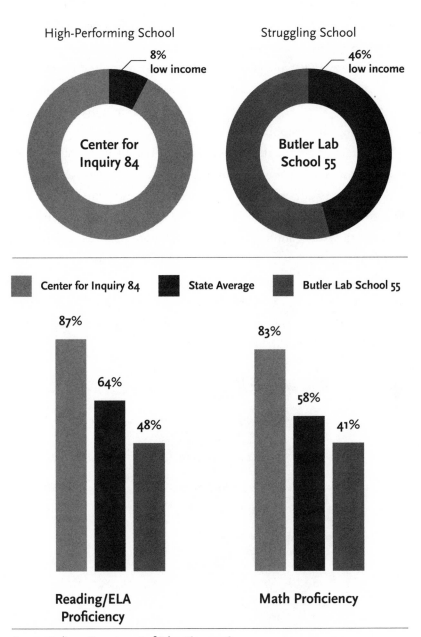

High-Performing School

8%
low income

Center for
Inquiry 84

Struggling School

46%
low income

Butler Lab
School 55

Center for Inquiry 84   State Average   Butler Lab School 55

87%

64%

48%

Reading/ELA
Proficiency

83%

58%

41%

Math Proficiency

Source: Indiana Department of Education, 2018–19

JACKSONVILLE:
Hendricks Avenue Elem. vs. Spring Park Elem.

Hendricks Avenue Elementary, one of Jacksonville's best elementary schools, is situated in the tony waterfront neighborhood of San Marco, near downtown. Parents gush about the school in online reviews and have admitted to paying $100,000 more than they wished for homes in the attendance area.[14] Pop singer Jason Mraz recently made a surprise appearance at the school.[15]

Just a mile-and-a-quarter away, at Spring Park Elementary, the news stories are starkly different. In November 2018, parents worried for their children's safety after a twenty-year-old man was shot in a playground near the school, with children nearby.[16] The geographical attendance zones of the two schools share a border of more than two miles along Route 1. But students at Spring Park are not free to cross Route 1 and transfer to the safer school. "You could apply," says the office staff. "But we are 100% full, so it's not likely. Really the only way is if you move into our neighborhood." But aren't the houses much more expensive in the Hendricks zone? "Yes, definitely."[17]

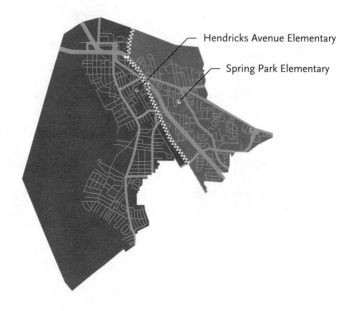

Hendricks Avenue Elementary

Spring Park Elementary

Percentage of Students

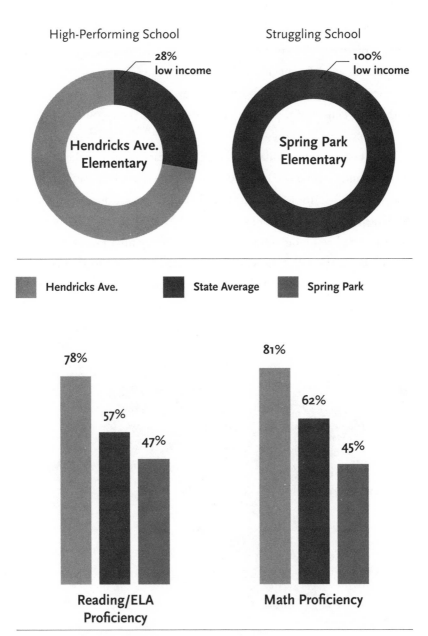

High-Performing School

Struggling School

28% low income

100% low income

Hendricks Ave. Elementary

Spring Park Elementary

Hendricks Ave. · State Average · Spring Park

78% · 57% · 47%

Reading/ELA Proficiency

81% · 62% · 45%

Math Proficiency

Source: Florida Department of Education, 2018–19

LOS ANGELES (Silver Lake):
Ivanhoe Elem. vs. Atwater Avenue Elem.

In Los Angeles, it's not enough to buy within the current attendance-zone boundaries of a coveted school. "If you are looking into real estate in order to attend a specific local school," writes Tanya Anton, the Los Angeles school admissions consultant, "my advice would be to land well within the center of the area, not on the periphery or outskirts of the attendance area."[18]

That's because schools like Ivanhoe Elementary in Silver Lake attract so many families who move into the zone that the school reaches capacity—and then the school-district officials redraw the boundaries to cut students out. "Recent population explosions in areas such as [Ivanhoe] have angered residents who thought they had paid a premium just to live within a school's footprint," reports Anton, "only to find out that boundaries had or will likely change to accommodate the incoming swell of students."

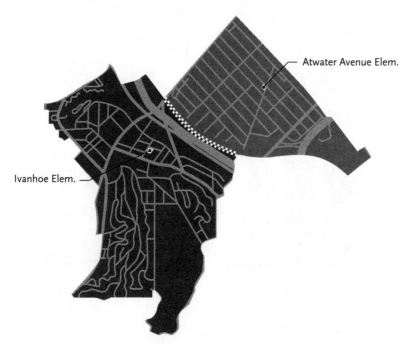

Atwater Avenue Elem.

Ivanhoe Elem.

Percentage of Students

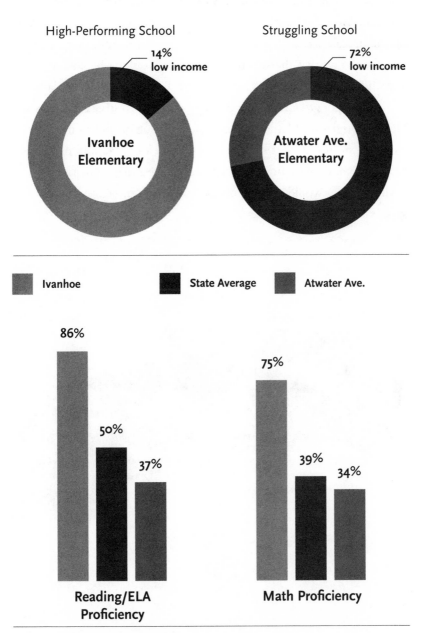

Source: California Department of Education, 2018–19

LOS ANGELES (Westside):
Canfield Ave. Elem. vs.Crescent Heights Blvd. Elem.

Canfield Avenue Elementary serves the neighborhood of Beverlywood on the upscale Westside of Los Angeles. The staff member who answers the phone says that the school is "full" and wouldn't be able to enroll any students who live across Bedford Street, which is the boundary that marks who goes to Canfield and who is assigned to struggling Crescent Heights Boulevard Elementary. But the meaning of "full" is not entirely clear. According to that same staff member, a new family paying the financial premium to move into the attendance zone on the right side of Bedford Street would not be turned away. "Even though we're full," she says, "we do have to take them."[19]

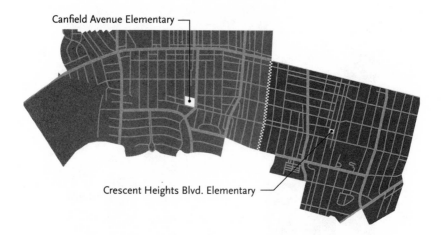

Canfield Avenue Elementary

Crescent Heights Blvd. Elementary

Percentage of Students

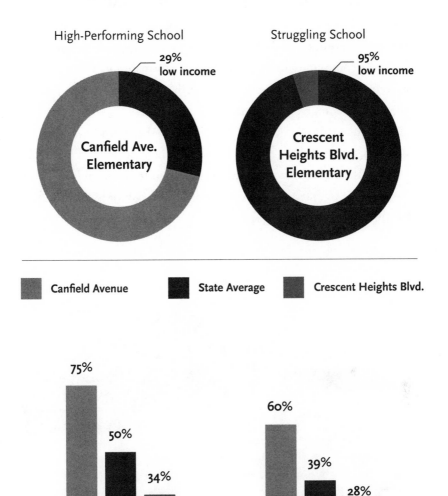

Source: California Department of Education, 2018–19

NEW YORK (Brooklyn):
PS 8 Robert Fulton vs. PS 307 Daniel Hale Williams

Two years ago, Brooklyn decided to redraw the attendance-zone boundaries around two highly segregated elementary schools in order to reduce community divisions and the performance gap between the two schools.[20] But, even after the change, the two schools remain starkly different in demographics and student performance.

Unlike many districts that have programs so that at least some out-of-zone students can gain access to better schools, high-achieving PS 8 is fully closed to the children living right outside its district-drawn boundaries. "We're zoned by our area," says a school staffer. "We only take students that are zoned for PS 8."[21]

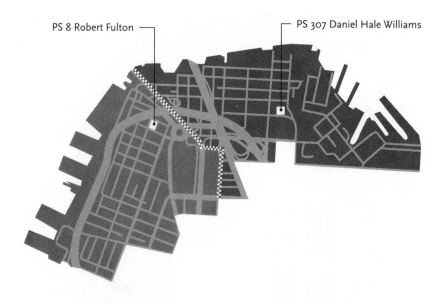

PS 8 Robert Fulton ⎯   ⎯ PS 307 Daniel Hale Williams

Percentage of Students

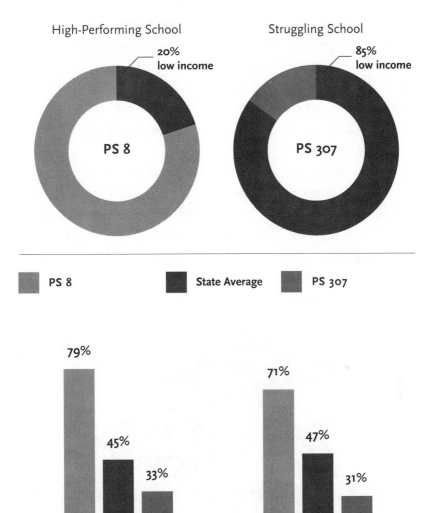

High-Performing School

Struggling School

20%
low income

85%
low income

PS 8

PS 307

PS 8   State Average   PS 307

79%

45%

33%

Reading/ELA
Proficiency

71%

47%

31%

Math Proficiency

Source: New York State Education Department, 2018–19

NEW YORK (Upper West Side):
PS 199 Jessie Isador Straus vs. Riverside School

On the Upper West Side of Manhattan, wealthy parents were in an uproar when school-district officials decided to redraw the attendance-zone boundaries for high-performing PS 199, leaving out portions of the prestigious Lincoln Towers apartment complex.[22] The irate parents launched a petition[23] asking the district to fund a building addition at PS 199, despite the fact that PS 191 (since renamed Riverside School), less than half a mile away, was struggling with empty seats.

After the district pushed through the attendance-boundary changes, some parents simply moved to regain access to PS 199. Yet many of the low-income families who now found themselves assigned to prestigious PS 199 apparently decided to stay at Riverside. "Just as it can be intimidating to be the only white child in a class, it can also be intimidating to be the only child of color in a class," school expert Clara Hemphill told the *New York Times*.[24]

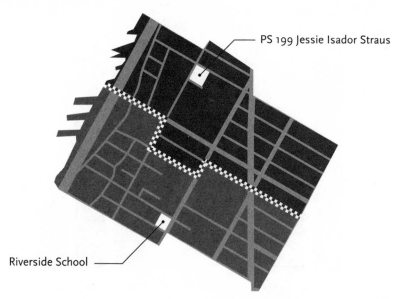

PS 199 Jessie Isador Straus

Riverside School

Percentage of Students

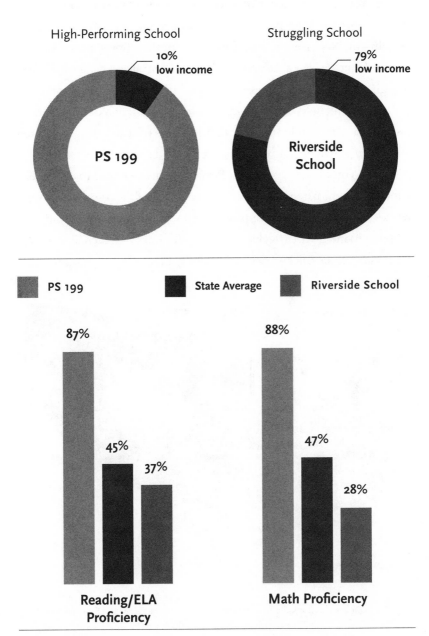

High-Performing School

10%
low income

PS 199

Struggling School

79%
low income

Riverside
School

PS 199   State Average   Riverside School

87%

45%

37%

**Reading/ELA
Proficiency**

88%

47%

28%

Math Proficiency

Source: New York State Education Department, 2018–19

OAKLAND: Peralta Elem. vs. Sankofa Academy

Lakisha Young is the executive director of Oakland REACH, a non-profit that coaches low-income parents on school selection. "During open enrollment," says Young, "you can theoretically choose any school in Oakland. But we have an access problem....There are such a small number of high-quality schools," she says. "People buy into those neighborhoods."

Peralta Elementary and Sankofa Academy are three blocks away from each other. One is full, and the other has "lots of space." Can you guess which one is which? The district has proposed merging the two schools at least two times since 2017,[25] but Peralta parents were able to defeat such efforts. A recent parent survey at Peralta—83% of the respondents were white—showed that 64% opposed the merger. Instead, Oakland now proposes to integrate struggling Sankofa with Kaiser Elementary, a school four miles up the hill and demographically more similar to Sankofa.[26]

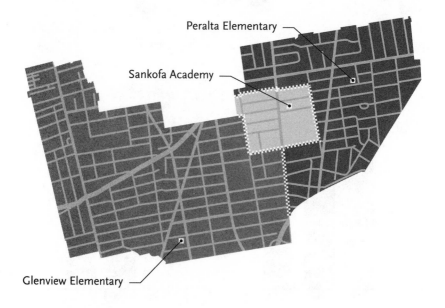

Note: The light-shaded areas indicate areas that are "shared" by the Peralta and Sankofa zones. Families in the rest of the Sankofa zone have "secondary" priority at Glenview Elementary, a school that is temporarily housed in the zone.

Percentage of Students

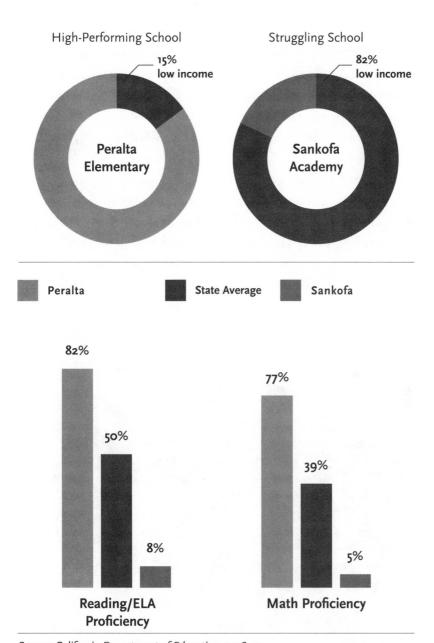

Source: *California Department of Education, 2018–19*

SAN DIEGO: Chesterton Elem. vs. Linda Vista Elem.

In San Diego, Linda Vista Elementary has been watching its enrollment numbers sag, partially because student performance is relatively weak— less than 30% of students are proficient in reading and math. In theory, those Linda Vista families could go less than a mile up the road to high-performing Chesterton Elementary, which serves many families who live in military housing nearby.

But Chesterton has the "littlest zone in the whole San Diego Unified," according to a staff member who recently answered the school telephone. He admitted that many parents from Linda Vista Elementary try to get their kids into the open slots for Chesterton. "Unfortunately, we only have so much space, so they end up at Linda Vista anyway."[27] Chesterton typically offers only eight to twelve seats per grade to children who live outside the zone. As a result, Linda Vista parents who want a better opportunity for their children have to look elsewhere—10% of families enroll their children in charter schools instead.[28]

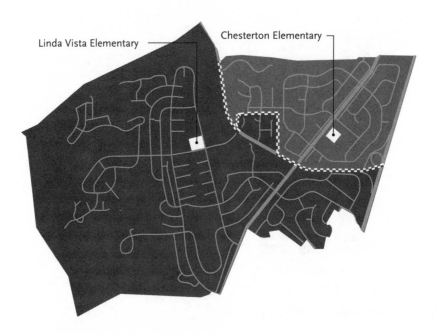

Linda Vista Elementary

Chesterton Elementary

Percentage of Students

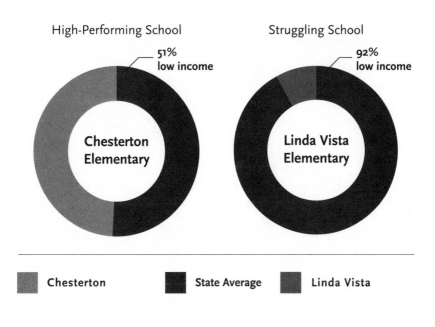

High-Performing School

51%
low income

Chesterton
Elementary

Struggling School

92%
low income

Linda Vista
Elementary

Chesterton   State Average   Linda Vista

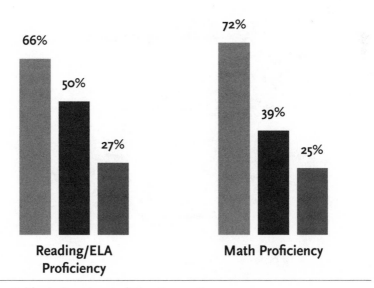

66%

50%

27%

Reading/ELA
Proficiency

72%

39%

25%

Math Proficiency

Source: California Department of Education, 2018–19

SAN JOSE:
James F. Smith Elem. vs. John J. Montgomery Elem.

Can a young family new to the foothills area of San Jose enroll their child in high-performing James F. Smith Elementary? "Well, you would have to live in our boundary," says a staff member at the school. There are "choice" options to apply to the school if you live outside the attendance zone. "But lately it seems to have been a long shot," the staff member laments. So the school is full? "Exactly."[29]

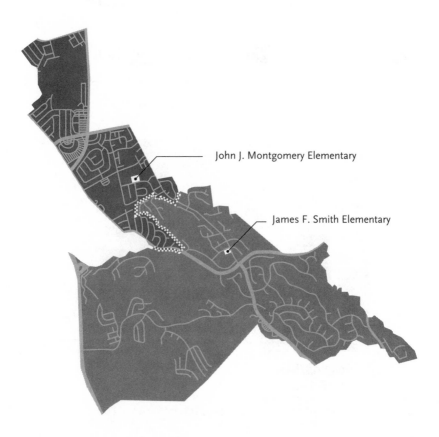

John J. Montgomery Elementary

James F. Smith Elementary

Percentage of Students

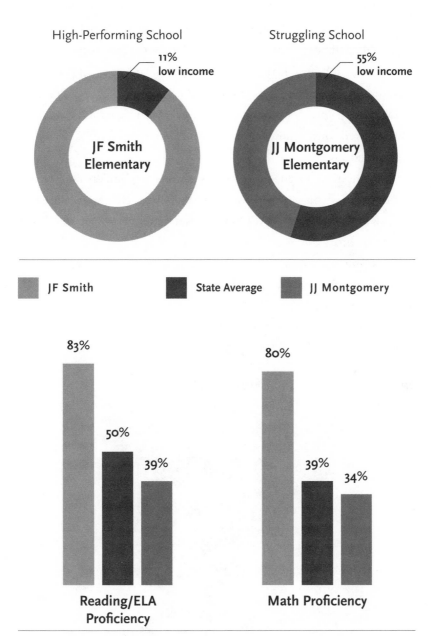

High-Performing School

11%
low income

JF Smith
Elementary

Struggling School

55%
low income

JJ Montgomery
Elementary

JF Smith   State Average   JJ Montgomery

83%

50%

39%

**Reading/ELA
Proficiency**

80%

39%

34%

Math Proficiency

Source: California Department of Education, 2018–19

SEATTLE: John Hay Elementary vs. Lowell Elementary

John Hay Elementary in Seattle is one of the most sought-after schools in the downtown area. "You want to be on the north side of Denny Way," says a staff member. "They're pretty strict" about the attendance areas, she says. And it's not possible to get into John Hay if you find that your home is within the zone that feeds into Lowell Elementary about a mile away, as John Hay is "pretty full." But they'll make room if a family moves into the preferred zone within the Queen Anne neighborhood. "Then you're guaranteed a spot."

If your home is assigned to Lowell, she says, "you don't really have any options unless you go to private schools." There are very few charter schools in Seattle, because Washington State didn't pass a charter school law until 2016.

"It is [unfair]," says the staff member at John Hay. "But you have to have boundaries somewhere. Otherwise no one would want to go to that school [Lowell]."[30]

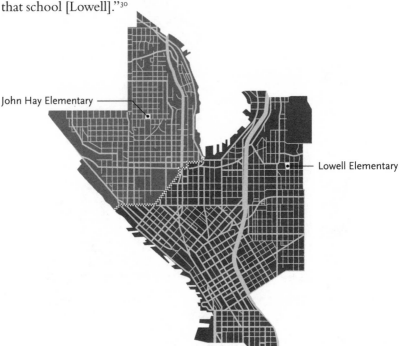

John Hay Elementary

Lowell Elementary

Percentage of Students

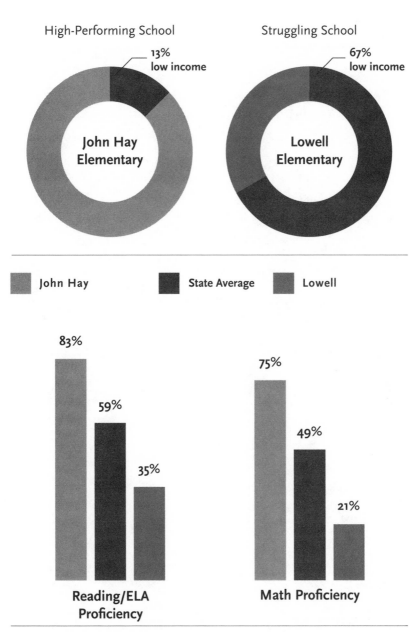

Source: Washington Office of the Superintendent of Public Instruction, 2018–19

APPENDIX B

STATE LAWS

STATES WHERE ATTENDANCE ZONES ARE VULNERABLE TO LEGAL CHALLENGE IN STATE COURTS

States promising public schools that are OPEN TO ALL

Alaska (*constitutional*)
Arizona (*constitutional*)
Arkansas (*statutory*)
Colorado (*statutory*)
Indiana (*constitutional*)
New Mexico (*constitutional*)
North Dakota (*constitutional*)
South Carolina (*constitutional*)
South Dakota (*constitutional*)

States promising EQUALITY OF EDUCATIONAL OPPORTUNITY

Louisiana (*constitutional*)
Montana (*constitutional*)
New Jersey (*Supreme Court*)
North Carolina (*constitutional*)
Tennessee (*Supreme Court*)

States where courts judge education to be a FUNDAMENTAL RIGHT

Alabama
Arizona
California
Connecticut
Kentucky
Minnesota
New Hampshire
North Carolina
North Dakota
Virginia
West Virginia
Wisconsin
Wyoming

Both (a) OPEN TO ALL or EQUAL OPPORTUNITY, and (b) a FUNDAMENTAL RIGHT

Arizona
North Carolina
North Dakota

States where some attendance zones appear to violate state civil rights statutes

Illinois

STATES IN WHICH...

(a) traditional public schools are allowed (or required) to discriminate against students based on residential address within the district, and (b) charter schools are forbidden from doing so

○ Allowed	● Required

State	○ ●	Traditional Public Schools	Charter Schools
AL	○	Ala. Code § 16-6F-5(a) (7)	Ala. Code § 16-6F-5
AK	○	Alaska Stat. § 14.60.010	Alaska Stat. § 14.03.265
AZ	○	Ariz. Rev. Stat. § 15-341	Ariz. Rev. Stat. § 15-184
CA	●	Cal. Ed. Code § 35160.5(b)	Cal. Ed. Code § 47605+
CO	○	Colo. Rev. Stat. § 22-36-101	Colo. Rev. Stat. § 22-30.5-104
CT	○	*No law found, but implicit*	Conn. Gen. Stat. § 10-66aa
DE	○	*No law found, but implicit*	Del. Code Title 14, § 506
DC	●	D.C. Mun. Regulations § 28:1-101	D.C. Mun. Regulations §5-E2001
HI	●	Haw. Rev. Stat. § 302A-1143	Haw. Rev. Stat.§ 302D-34+
IL	●	105 Ill. Comp. Stat. § 5/10-21.3	105 Ill. Comp. Stat. § 27A-4★
IN	○	Ind. Code § 20-25-4-12	Ind. Code § 20-24-5-5
KY	○	*No law found, but implicit*	Ky. Rev. Stat. § 160.1592+
ME	○	Me. Stat.Title 20-A § 1001	Me. Stat.Title 20-A § 1001+
MI	○	*No law found, but implicit*	Mich. Comp. Laws 380.504
MS	●	Miss. Code § 37-15-13	Miss. Code § 37-28-23
NV	○	Nev. Rev. Stat. § 388.040	Nev. Rev. Stat. § 388A.453
NH	○	N.H. Rev. Stat. § 194-D:2	N.H. Rev. Stat. § 194-B:2(IV)
NJ	○	*No law found, but implicit*	N.J. Rev. Stat. § 18A:36A-8
NM	●	N.M. Stat. § 22-1-4(E)	N.M. Stat. § 22-8B-4.1
NY	○	*No law found, but implicit*	N.Y. Educ. Law § 2853
NC	○	N.C. Gen. Stat. § 115C-47	N.C. Gen. Stat. § 115C-218.45
OH	○	Ohio Rev. Code § 3319.01	Ohio Rev. Code § 3314.06
OR	○	*No law found, but implicit*	Ore. Rev. Stat. § 338.125+
PA	●	24 Pa. Cons. Stat. § 1310	24 Pa. Cons. Stat. § 1701-51
TN	○	Tenn. Code § 49-6-3103	Tenn. Code § 49-13-113+
TX	○	Tex. Educ. Code § 25.031	Tex. Educ. Code § 12.117
VA	○	Va. Code § 22.1-79	Va. Code § 22.1-212.6
WA	○	*No law found, but implicit*	Wash. Rev. Code §28A.710.050
WI	○	Wis. Stat. § 118.51	Wis. Stat. § 118.40

+ Traditional public schools that *convert* to charter status are required to retain the existing attendance zone and discriminate based on residential address in enrollment decisions. All other charters are forbidden from discriminating against students based on their residential address within the district. Oregon allows charter schools to use an attendance zone if they are replacing a closed district school.

★ The Illinois legislature specifically exempts only the Chicago Public Schools from this ban on geographical discrimination: "Priority may be given to pupils residing within the charter school's attendance boundary, if a boundary has been designated by the board of education in a city having a population exceeding 500,000."

STATES THAT EXPLICITLY CRIMINALIZE USING AN INCORRECT ADDRESS FOR PUBLIC SCHOOL ENROLLMENT

State	Statute
Arkansas	Ark. Code § 6-18-02
District of Columbia	DC Municipal Regulations § 5-A5012
Illinois	105 Ill. Comp. Stat. § 10-20.12b
Indiana	Ind. Code § 20-33-8-17
Maryland	Md. Code, Ed. Law § 7-101(3)
Massachusetts	Mass. Gen. Laws Title 12 ch. 76 § 5
Michigan	Mich. Comp. Laws § 380.1812
Minnesota	Minn. Stat. § 120A.26
Missouri	Mo. Rev. Stat. § 167.020
New Jersey	N.J. Rev. Stat. 18A § 38-1
North Carolina	N.C. Gen. Stat. § 115C-366(a3)
Oklahoma	Okla. Stat. Title 70 § 1-113
Pennsylvania	24 Pa. Cons. Stat. § 13-130
South Carolina	S.C. Code § 59-63-32
Texas	Tex. Educ. Code Title 2 Sub. B § 25.001 and Pen. Code § 37.10
Virginia	Va. Code § 22.1-264.1

STATES WHERE ATTENDANCE ZONES MAY BE VULNERABLE TO LEGAL CHALLENGE IN STATE COURTS

ALABAMA

OPEN TO ALL?	No
EQUAL EDUCATIONAL OPPORTUNITY?	No
FUNDAMENTAL RIGHT?	Yes—*Opinion of the Justices No. 338.624 So. 2d 107, 157 (1993)*

STATE CONSTITUTION

Art. 14 § 256. The legislature shall establish, organize, and maintain a liberal system of public schools throughout the state for the benefit of the children thereof between the ages of seven and twenty-one years.... Separate schools shall be provided for white and colored children, and no child of either race shall be permitted to attend a school of the other race.

NOTES

In Alabama, attendance zones could be vulnerable to an equal protection challenge and strict scrutiny review, because the AL Supreme Court has ruled education to be a fundamental right.

Alabama's constitution still specifies separate schools for black and white students, though this provision cannot be legally enforced since it violates the ruling in *Brown v. Board of Education.*

OPEN ENROLLMENT

WITHIN-DISTRICT None found.
CROSS-DISTRICT None found.

STATE LAW ESTABLISHING ATTENDANCE ZONES

None found.

STATE LAWS CRIMINALIZING USE OF INCORRECT ADDRESS

None found.

CHARTER SCHOOL ADMISSIONS

Charter schools are forbidden from discriminating against students based on their residential address within the school district. The exception is conversion charter schools, which must give enrollment priority to students who reside in the former attendance area of the school. All charter schools must be open to any student who resides in the state. If applications exceed capacity, schools must give enrollment priority to students who reside in the district jurisdiction where the charter school is located. Ala. Code § 16-6F-5

ALASKA

OPEN TO ALL?	Yes—*constitutional*
EQUAL EDUCATIONAL OPPORTUNITY?	No
FUNDAMENTAL RIGHT?	No

STATE CONSTITUTION

Art. 7 § 1. The legislature shall by general law establish and maintain a system of public schools open to all children of the State, and may provide for other public educational institutions.

NOTES

In Alaska, attendance zones could be vulnerable to a challenge based on the promise in the state constitution that the public schools be "open to all."

STATE LAW ESTABLISHING ATTENDANCE ZONES

Alaska appears to give the state the ultimate power to determine attendance areas, rather than local districts. Alaska Stat. 14.60.010: "'attendance area' means the geographic area designated by the department to be served by a school." Also see 4 Alaska Administrative Code (AAC) 06.027: "The board may establish attendance areas without respect to district lines."

OPEN ENROLLMENT

WITHIN-DISTRICT Alaska's only open-enrollment statutes relate to transfers of students from persistently dangerous schools. Per 4 AAC 06.210: "A district that contains a school that has been designated persistently dangerous shall (1) within 10 days after the department designates the school, provide all parents of students who attend the school notice that the (A) school has been designated as persistently dangerous; and (B) parent may, within 30 days after the notice is sent, request that the district transfer the student to the parent's choice of one of two or more safe schools within the district."
CROSS-DISTRICT None found.

STATE LAWS CRIMINALIZING USE OF INCORRECT ADDRESS

None found.

CHARTER SCHOOL ADMISSIONS

Charter schools are forbidden from discriminating against students based on their residential address. Alaska Stat. 14.03.265

ARIZONA

OPEN TO ALL?	Yes— *constitutional*
EQUAL EDUCATIONAL OPPORTUNITY?	No
FUNDAMENTAL RIGHT?	Yes—*Shofstall v. Hollins* (1973)

STATE CONSTITUTION

Art. 11 § 1A. The legislature shall enact such laws as shall provide for the establishment and maintenance of a general and uniform public school system.... Art. 11 § 6. The legislature shall provide for a system of common schools by which a free school shall be established and maintained in every school district for at least six months in each year, which school shall be open to all pupils between the ages of six and twenty-one years.

NOTES

In Arizona, attendance zones could be vulnerable on two legal fronts: (1) a challenge based on the promise in the state constitution that the public schools be "open to all," and (2) an equal protection challenge with strict scrutiny review, because the AZ Supreme Court has ruled education to be a fundamental right.

STATE LAW ESTABLISHING ATTENDANCE ZONES

None found.

OPEN ENROLLMENT

WITHIN-DISTRICT None found.
CROSS-DISTRICT None found.

STATE LAWS CRIMINALIZING USE OF INCORRECT ADDRESS

None found.

CHARTER SCHOOL ADMISSIONS

Charter schools not allowed use geographic enrollment preferences. § 15-184 establishes that charter schools must admit all students who submit a timely application unless applications exceed capacity, in which case a lottery must be held. Charter schools can give admissions preference to returning students, siblings of students, children in foster care or homeless youth, and children of school employees and the school's governing board.

ARKANSAS

OPEN TO ALL?	Yes—*statutory, not constitutional*
EQUAL EDUCATIONAL OPPORTUNITY?	No
FUNDAMENTAL RIGHT?	No

STATE CONSTITUTION

Art. 14 § 1. Intelligence and virtue being the safeguards of liberty and the bulwark of a free and good government, the State shall ever maintain a general, suitable and efficient system of free public schools and shall adopt all suitable means to secure to the people the advantages and opportunities of education.

NOTES

In Arkansas, attendance zones could be vulnerable to a challenge based on the statutory promise in Ark. Code § 6-18-202 that public schools need to be "open … to all persons in this state between the ages of 5 and 21."

STATE LAW ESTABLISHING ATTENDANCE ZONES

None found.

OPEN ENROLLMENT

WITHIN-DISTRICT Ark. Code § 6-18-202: "The public schools of any school district in this state shall be open and free through completion of the secondary program to all persons in this state between five (5) and twenty-one (21) years of age whose parents, foster parents, legal guardians, or other persons having lawful control of the person under an order of a court reside within the school district and to all persons between those ages who have been legally transferred to the district for education purposes."

CROSS-DISTRICT Ark. Code § 6-18-1903 requires each school district to establish a public school choice program, although districts may opt out using a claim of lack of capacity and generally have broad leeway to limit the program. School choice transfers out of a district may not exceed 3% of the previous year's district enrollment, less any transfers into the district.

STATE LAWS CRIMINALIZING USE OF INCORRECT ADDRESS

Ark. Code § 6-18-202 states that school districts may require parents or guardians to sign oaths attesting to their residence and must immediately bar students found not to be residents of the district from attending.

CHARTER SCHOOL ADMISSIONS

Charter schools are allowed to establish an attendance area and are allowed to discriminate against students based on their residential address. Ark. Code § 6-23-306

CALIFORNIA

OPEN TO ALL?	No
EQUAL EDUCATIONAL OPPORTUNITY?	No
FUNDAMENTAL RIGHT?	Yes—*Serrano v. Priest* (1971)

STATE CONSTITUTION

Article IX, § 5. The Legislature shall provide for a system of common schools by which a free school shall be kept up and supported in each district at least six months in every year, after the first year in which a school has been established.

NOTES

In California, attendance zones could be vulnerable to an equal protection challenge and strict scrutiny review, because the CA Supreme Court has ruled education to be a "fundamental interest," which has been interpreted to mean that education is a fundamental right in CA. However, such a challenge will have to contend with § 7 of Art. I of the state constitution, which was passed as a ballot Proposition 1 in 1979 and which forbids the state courts from applying a standard of strict scrutiny in the limited domains of "pupil school assignment or pupil transportation." The amendment was passed to block courts from implementing desegregation busing schemes, which were very unpopular with the CA public. It is unclear whether § 7 would survive a court challenge today.

Because K-12 education is primarily funded by the state, the case for eliminating district boundaries is more compelling in CA than in most other states. The Districts of Choice program—expiring in 2023—is a step toward allowing all students to attend the district of their choosing. There is also a favorable legislative precedent, because students were originally assigned to community colleges by residential address, but the state legislature opened up all community colleges to all students in 1987.

STATE LAW ESTABLISHING ATTENDANCE ZONES

The open enrollment law implicitly requires zones by stating that students have access to any school within their district, but not if a student from the attendance area will be displaced.

OPEN ENROLLMENT

WITHIN-DISTRICT CA Education Code § 35160.5(b). Mandated by state law, but discrimination required based on address of residence: No pupil who resides in the attendance area of a school shall be displaced by pupils transferring from outside the attendance area.

CROSS-DISTRICT CA Ed Code § 46600–46607, 48204(b), 48300–48316: Can be denied by either the resident district or the non-resident district. Requires student to get permit to cross district lines (waived for military personnel).

§ 48301 establishes a temporary "district of choice" program in which state funding follows students to selected districts that choose to participate. A permit from the resident district is not required. Expires in 2023.

STATE LAWS CRIMINALIZING USE OF INCORRECT ADDRESS

None found.

CHARTER SCHOOL ADMISSIONS

Most charter schools are forbidden from discriminating against students based on their residential address. But a charter school that is converted to charter from an existing public school is required to discriminate on the same basis: "Admission to a charter school shall not be determined according to the place of residence of the pupil, or of the pupil's parent or legal guardian, within this state, except that an existing public school converting partially or entirely to a charter school under this part shall adopt and maintain a policy giving admission preference to pupils who reside within the former attendance area of that public school." CA Ed Code § 47605.

COLORADO

OPEN TO ALL?	Yes—*statutory, not constitutional*
EQUAL EDUCATIONAL OPPORTUNITY?	No
FUNDAMENTAL RIGHT?	No

STATE CONSTITUTION

Art. 9 § 2. The general assembly shall, as soon as practicable, provide for the establishment and maintenance of a thorough and uniform system of free public schools throughout the state, wherein all residents of the state, between the ages of six and twenty-one years, may be educated gratuitously. One or more public schools shall be maintained in each school district within the state, at least three months in each year; any school district failing to have such school shall not be entitled to receive any portion of the school fund for that year.

NOTES

In Colorado, attendance zones could be vulnerable to a challenge based on the statutory promise in Colo. Rev. Stat. § 22-1- 102 that "every public school shall be open for the admission of all children ... residing in that district."

STATE LAW ESTABLISHING ATTENDANCE ZONES

The open enrollment law implicitly allows attendance zones by stating that students have access to any school within their district, but application can be denied if the school or program is full with students from the preferred enrollment area.

STATE LAWS CRIMINALIZING USE OF INCORRECT ADDRESS

None found.

OPEN ENROLLMENT

WITHIN-DISTRICT Colo. Rev. Stat. § 22-36-101 requires every school district to establish policies and procedures for students to apply to "particular programs or schools within such school district." Schools may give enrollment preference to transfer students who are struggling academically and from schools subject to restructuring or turnaround plans. Schools may deny permission to transfer when programs or schools lack the capacity.
CROSS-DISTRICT Same law cited above applies to cross-district transfers.

CHARTER SCHOOL ADMISSIONS

Charter schools appear to be forbidden from discriminating against students based on their residential address within the school district. Each charter school must be open to every child living in the district where the school is located, and enrollment decisions must be made in a "nondiscriminatory manner." Colo. Rev. Stat. 22-30.5-104

CONNECTICUT

OPEN TO ALL?	No
EQUAL EDUCATIONAL OPPORTUNITY?	No
FUNDAMENTAL RIGHT?	Yes—*Horton v. Meskill* (1977)

STATE CONSTITUTION

Art. 8 § 1. There shall always be free public elementary and secondary schools in the state. The general assembly shall implement this principle by appropriate legislation.

NOTES

In Connecticut, attendance zones could be vulnerable to an equal protection challenge and strict scrutiny review, because the CT Supreme Court has ruled education to be a fundamental right.

STATE LAW ESTABLISHING ATTENDANCE ZONES

None found.

STATE LAWS CRIMINALIZING USE OF INCORRECT ADDRESS

None found.

OPEN ENROLLMENT

WITHIN-DISTRICT Conn. Gen. Stat. § 10-221e grants local and regional school boards the power to establish within-district open enrollment programs at their own discretion: "Under such programs parents may select the public school which their child will attend provided the school is in the school district in which the child resides."

CROSS-DISTRICT Required for certain specified districts. Does not appear that resident district can deny a transfer. Conn. Gen. Stat. § 10-266aa(b).

CHARTER SCHOOL ADMISSIONS

All charter schools are forbidden from discriminating against students based on their residential address and must use a lottery. Conn. Gen. Stat. § 10-66aa.

ILLINOIS

OPEN TO ALL?	No
EQUAL EDUCATIONAL OPPORTUNITY?	No
FUNDAMENTAL RIGHT?	No

STATE CONSTITUTION

Art. X § 1. A fundamental goal of the People of the State is the educational development of all persons to the limits of their capacities. The State shall provide for an efficient system of high quality public educational institutions and services. Education in public schools through the secondary level shall be free. There may be such other free education as the General Assembly provides by law. The State has the primary responsibility for financing the system of public education.

NOTES

In Illinois, a challenge to attendance zones would focus on highly segregated schools like Lincoln Elementary and Manierre Elementary. State law (ILCS Chap. 105 §10-21.3) requires the district to redraw lines to reduce racial segregation. In the Old Town neighborhood of the Chicago Public Schools, there is substantial evidence that the district has gone to great lengths to avoid redrawing the zones in a way that would reduce segregation. Chicago Public Schools even went so far as to approve a $19 million addition to the Lincoln Elementary facility, so that students in the Lincoln attendance zone would not be reassigned to empty classroom seats in Manierre.

STATE LAW ESTABLISHING ATTENDANCE ZONES

ILCS Chap. 105 §10-21.3 requires school districts to periodically re-draw attendance boundaries "in a manner which will take into consideration the prevention of segregation and the elimination of separation of children in public schools because of color, race or nationality."

OPEN ENROLLMENT

WITHIN-DISTRICT §10-21.3a of ILCS Chap. 105 requires districts to establish a policy for allowing a student to transfer to another attendance zone but only if space is available.

CROSS-DISTRICT None found.

STATE LAWS CRIMINALIZING USE OF INCORRECT ADDRESS

ILCS Chap. 105 §10-20.12b states that a person who enrolls a student in a district of which the student is not a resident can be held liable for back tuition if the student attended on a tuition-free basis.

CHARTER SCHOOL ADMISSIONS

ILCS Chap. 105 § 27A-4 establishes that charter schools must use a lottery to enroll students if applications exceed capacity. However, in cities with population over 500,000 (i.e., only in Chicago), the school may give priority to students residing within an attendance boundary designated by the board of education.

INDIANA

OPEN TO ALL?	Yes— *constitutional*
EQUAL EDUCATIONAL OPPORTUNITY?	No
FUNDAMENTAL RIGHT?	No

STATE CONSTITUTION

Art. 8 § 1. Knowledge and learning, generally diffused throughout a community, being essential to the preservation of a free government; it should be the duty of the General Assembly to encourage, by all suitable means, moral, intellectual scientific, and agricultural improvement; and provide, by law, for a general and uniform system of Common Schools, wherein tuition shall be without charge, and equally open to all.

NOTES

In Indiana, attendance zones could be vulnerable to a challenge based on the promise in the state constitution that the public schools be "equally open to all."

STATE LAW ESTABLISHING ATTENDANCE ZONES

Ind. Code § 20-25-4-12 states that boards of school commissioners "may ... divide the city into districts for school attendance purposes."

OPEN ENROLLMENT

WITHIN-DISTRICT Ind. Code § 20-25-7-1 (applies only to Indianapolis): "The school city shall offer a parental choice program that allows a parent the opportunity to choose the school in the school city that the parent's child will attend." The school can deny admission because of "building capacity."

CROSS-DISTRICT Ind. Code § 20-26-11-5 states that parents or guardians may request transfer for their student to a different school corporation, but requests may be denied by either the sending or receiving district.

STATE LAWS CRIMINALIZING USE OF INCORRECT ADDRESS

Ind. Code § 20-33-8-17: "A student may be expelled from school if the student's legal settlement is not in the attendance area of the school corporation where the student is enrolled."

CHARTER SCHOOL ADMISSIONS

All charter schools are forbidden from discriminating against students based on their residential address and must use a lottery. Ind. Code § 20-24-5-5

KENTUCKY

OPEN TO ALL? No

EQUAL EDUCATIONAL OPPORTUNITY? No

FUNDAMENTAL RIGHT? Yes—*Rose v. Council for Better Education* (1989)

STATE CONSTITUTION

§ 183. The General Assembly shall, by appropriate legislation, provide for an efficient system of common schools throughout the State.

NOTES

In Kentucky, attendance zones could be vulnerable to an equal protection challenge and strict scrutiny review, because the KY Supreme Court has ruled education to be a fundamental right.

STATE LAW ESTABLISHING ATTENDANCE ZONES

None found.

STATE LAWS CRIMINALIZING USE OF INCORRECT ADDRESS

None found.

OPEN ENROLLMENT

WITHIN-DISTRICT None found.
CROSS-DISTRICT Voluntary for districts. Requires agreement between sending and receiving district. Ky. Rev. Stat. § 158.120

CHARTER SCHOOL ADMISSIONS

Charter schools are forbidden from discriminating against students based on their residential address within the school district. Conversion charter schools must give enrollment priority to students who reside within the school district's jurisdictional boundaries. Ky. Rev. Stat. § 160.1592

LOUISIANA

OPEN TO ALL?	No
EQUAL EDUCATIONAL OPPORTUNITY?	Yes
FUNDAMENTAL RIGHT?	No

STATE CONSTITUTION

Art. 8 Preamble. The goal of the public educational system is to provide learning environments and experiences, at all stages of human development, that are humane, just, and designed to promote excellence in order that every individual may be afforded an equal opportunity to develop to his full potential.

Art. 8 § 1. The legislature shall provide for the education of the people of the state and shall establish and maintain a public educational system.

NOTES

In Louisiana, attendance zones could be vulnerable to a challenge based on the promise in the state constitution that the public schools provide "equal opportunity" for every individual.

A separate set of laws apply to the Recovery District which was created in the aftermath of Hurricane Katrina. The legislature requires that the students in the Recovery District be assigned to schools "without regard to the attendance zones" and that schools have open enrollment policies for "the enrollment of students in reasonable proximity to the neighborhoods where concentrations of students reside." La. Stat. Title 17 § 10.7.

STATE LAW ESTABLISHING ATTENDANCE ZONES

No laws, but regulations permit attendance zones. LA Administrative Code Title 28 Part CXV § 303: "Each city and parish school board shall have full and final authority and responsibility for the assignment, transfer and continuance of all students among and within the public schools within its jurisdiction."

STATE LAWS CRIMINALIZING USE OF INCORRECT ADDRESS

None found.

CHARTER SCHOOL ADMISSIONS

Charter schools are allowed to establish "geographic boundaries" and grant "preference for enrollment" to those living within the boundaries. La. Stat. Title 17 § 3991.

OPEN ENROLLMENT

WITHIN-DISTRICT Required for districts but only when "space available" and when child lives within one mile of desired school. Does not apply to Orleans Parish. La. Stat. Title 17 § 221.2.

CROSS-DISTRICT Allowed. But both sending and receiving district must approve. La. Rev. Stat. Title 17 § 105

MINNESOTA

OPEN TO ALL?	No
EQUAL EDUCATIONAL OPPORTUNITY?	No
FUNDAMENTAL RIGHT?	Yes—*Skeen v. Minnesota* (1993)

STATE CONSTITUTION

Art. 13 § 1. The stability of a republican form of government depending mainly upon the intelligence of the people, it is the duty of the legislature to establish a general and uniform system of public schools. The legislature shall make such provisions by taxation or otherwise as will secure a thorough and efficient system of public schools throughout the state.

NOTES

In Minnesota, attendance zones could be vulnerable to an equal protection challenge and strict scrutiny review, because the MN Supreme Court has ruled education to be a fundamental right.

Minn. Stat. § 120A.36: "Attendance at a particular public school is a privilege not a right for a pupil."

STATE LAW ESTABLISHING ATTENDANCE ZONES

Minn. Stat. § 123B.02 (2): "The [independent school district] board may establish and organize and alter and discontinue such grades or schools as it may deem advisable and assign to each school and grade a proper number of pupils."

OPEN ENROLLMENT

WITHIN-DISTRICT None found.
CROSS-DISTRICT Minn. Stat. § 124D.03 establishes a cross-district open enrollment program, but districts may limit open enrollment slots to no more than 1% of students in each grade level or the number of its own residents enrolled in nonresident districts at a particular grade level. Where school districts receive more applications than spaces, a lottery is required.

STATE LAWS CRIMINALIZING USE OF INCORRECT ADDRESS

Minn. Stat. § 120A.26 states that parents found to be sending their child to a school the student does not have a right to attend based on residency (per § 120A.22) in the school district may be subject to a "fact-finding and mediation process" and ultimately prosecution for a misdemeanor if mediation fails.

CHARTER SCHOOL ADMISSIONS

Charter schools are forbidden from discriminating against students based on their residential address. The exception is schools that serve a majority of students who are members of underserved populations; these schools are allowed to limit enrollment to a specific "geographic area." Minn. Stat. § 124E.11

MONTANA

OPEN TO ALL?	No
EQUAL EDUCATIONAL OPPORTUNITY?	Yes
FUNDAMENTAL RIGHT?	No

STATE CONSTITUTION

Art. 10 § 1. It is the goal of the people to establish a system of education which will develop the full educational potential of each person. Equality of educational opportunity is guaranteed to each person of the state....The legislature shall provide a basic system of free quality public elementary and secondary schools.

NOTES

In Montana, attendance zones could be vulnerable to a challenge based on the promise in the state constitution that "equality of educational opportunity is guaranteed to each person of the state."

A state district court ruled that education is a "fundamental right," but—in *Helena Elementary School District v. State*—the MT Supreme Court specifically declined to confirm or overrule the lower court's finding.

STATE LAW ESTABLISHING ATTENDANCE ZONES

None found.

STATE LAWS CRIMINALIZING USE OF INCORRECT ADDRESS

None found.

OPEN ENROLLMENT

WITHIN-DISTRICT None found.
CROSS-DISTRICT Voluntary for districts. Both sending and receiving district must approve. Mandatory under certain limited conditions. Mont. Code § 20-5-320

CHARTER SCHOOL ADMISSIONS

No charter school law. But Montana Administrative Code rule 10.55.604 allows districts to petition for the creation of charter schools and requires that they must have "unrestricted, open student access." There are very few charter schools in Montana.

NEW HAMPSHIRE

OPEN TO ALL?	No
EQUAL EDUCATIONAL OPPORTUNITY?	No
FUNDAMENTAL RIGHT?	Yes—*Claremont School District v. Governor* (1997)

STATE CONSTITUTION

Part 2 Art. 83. It shall be the duty of the legislators and magistrates, in all future periods of this government, to cherish the interest of literature and the sciences, and all seminaries and public schools, to encourage private and public institutions, rewards, and immunities for the promotion of agriculture, arts, sciences, commerce, trades, manufactures, and natural history of the country; to countenance and inculcate the principles of humanity and general benevolence, public and private charity, industry and economy, honesty and punctuality, sincerity, sobriety, and all social affections, and generous sentiments, among the people...

NOTES

In New Hampshire, attendance zones could be vulnerable to an equal protection challenge and strict scrutiny review, because the NH Supreme Court has ruled education to be a fundamental right.

N.H. Rev. Stat. § 193:3 "Any person having custody of a child may apply to the school board for relief if the person thinks the attendance of the child at the school to which such child has been assigned will result in a manifest educational hardship to the child."

STATE LAW ESTABLISHING ATTENDANCE ZONES

Attendance zones are implicitly allowed by open enrollment law. N.H. Rev. Stat. § 194-D:2

OPEN ENROLLMENT

WITHIN-DISTRICT Voluntary for districts. Significant flexibility afforded to districts in enrollment policies. N.H. Rev. Stat. § 194-D:2

CROSS-DISTRICT Voluntary for districts. Resident district does not appear to have the right to deny a transfer. N.H. Rev. Stat. § 194-D:2

STATE LAWS CRIMINALIZING USE OF INCORRECT ADDRESS

None found.

CHARTER SCHOOL ADMISSIONS

Charter schools are forbidden from discriminating against students based on their residential address within the school district. But charters are required to grant an enrollment preference to students living within the jurisdictional boundaries. N.H. Rev. Stat. § 194-B:2(IV)

NEW JERSEY

OPEN TO ALL?	No
EQUAL EDUCATIONAL OPPORTUNITY?	Yes—*Robinson v. Cahill* (1973)
FUNDAMENTAL RIGHT?	No

STATE CONSTITUTION

Art. 8 § 4 (1). The Legislature shall provide for the maintenance and support of a thorough and efficient system of free public schools for the instruction of all the children in the State between the ages of five and eighteen years.

NOTES

In New Jersey, attendance zones could be vulnerable to a challenge based on the NJ Supreme Court's ruling that the state constitution requires "equal educational opportunity for children."

STATE LAW ESTABLISHING ATTENDANCE ZONES

None found.

OPEN ENROLLMENT

WITHIN-DISTRICT Limited programs focused on "renaissance schools" for high-risk populations. N.J. Rev. Stat. Title 18A § 36C-2.

CROSS-DISTRICT Voluntary for districts. Transfers do not appear to require permission from the resident district. Transfers can be rejected due to lack of capacity. N.J. Rev. Stat. Title 18A § 36B-16

STATE LAWS CRIMINALIZING USE OF INCORRECT ADDRESS

N.J. Rev. Stat. Title 18A § 38-1 states that school is free to any child who lives in the district or lives with an adult resident of the district provided that the resident provide a sworn affidavit that the child resides with the person because the parents or legal guardian cannot care for the child and not for the purpose of receiving a free education in that district. Violators can be fined $25–100.

CHARTER SCHOOL ADMISSIONS

Charter schools are forbidden from discriminating against students based on their residential address within the school district. But charters are required to grant an enrollment preference to students living within the jurisdictional boundaries. N.J. Rev. Stat. Title 18A § 36A-8

NEW MEXICO

OPEN TO ALL?	Yes— *constitutional*
EQUAL EDUCATIONAL OPPORTUNITY?	No
FUNDAMENTAL RIGHT?	No

STATE CONSTITUTION

Art. 12 § 1. A uniform system of free public schools sufficient for the education of, and open to, all the children of school age in the state shall be established and maintained.

NOTES

In New Mexico, attendance zones could be vulnerable to a challenge based on the promise in the state constitution that the public schools be "open to all the children of school age in the state."

STATE LAW ESTABLISHING ATTENDANCE ZONES

"A local school board shall adopt and promulgate rules governing enrollment and re-enrollment at public schools other than charter schools within the school district. These rules shall include: (1) definition of the school district boundary and the boundaries of attendance areas for each public school." N.M. Stat. § 22-1-4(E)

OPEN ENROLLMENT

WITHIN-DISTRICT Voluntary program for districts that specifically allows for geographic enrollment preferences within the district. N.M. Stat. § 22-12-5(B): "Local school boards may permit school-age persons to transfer to a school outside the child's attendance zone but within the school district when there are sufficient school accommodations to provide for them."
CROSS-DISTRICT Voluntary for districts. Permission of resident district not required. "Local school boards may admit school-age persons who do not live within the school district to the public schools within the school district when there are sufficient school accommodations to provide for them." N.M. Stat. § 22-12-5(A)

STATE LAWS CRIMINALIZING USE OF INCORRECT ADDRESS

None found.

CHARTER SCHOOL ADMISSIONS

Charter schools are forbidden from discriminating against students based on their residential address within the school district. But charters are required to grant an enrollment preference to students living within the jurisdictional boundaries. N.M. Stat. § 22-8B-4.1

NORTH CAROLINA

OPEN TO ALL?	No
EQUAL EDUCATIONAL OPPORTUNITY?	Yes
FUNDAMENTAL RIGHT?	Yes—*Leandro v. State* (1997)

STATE CONSTITUTION

Art. 9 § 1. Religion, morality, and knowledge being necessary to good government and the happiness of mankind, schools, libraries, and the means of education shall forever be encouraged.

Art. 9 § 2. The General Assembly shall provide by taxation and otherwise for a general and uniform system of free public schools, which shall be maintained at least nine months in every year, and wherein equal opportunities shall be provided for all students.

NOTES

In North Carolina, attendance zones could be vulnerable on two legal fronts: (1) a challenge based on the promise in the state constitution that the public schools provide "equal opportunities ... for all students," and (2) an equal protection challenge with strict scrutiny review, because the NC Supreme Court has ruled education to be a fundamental right.

STATE LAW ESTABLISHING ATTENDANCE ZONES

N.C.Gen. Stat. § 115C-47: "Local boards of education shall have the power or duty: (3) To Divide Local School Administrative Units into Attendance Areas. – Local boards of education shall have authority to divide their various units into attendance areas without regard to district lines.

OPEN ENROLLMENT

WITHIN-DISTRICT Voluntary program for districts with significant local discretion, allowing districts to assign children to a school outside their attendance area "for any other reason which the board of education in its sole discretion deems sufficient." N.C. Gen. Stat. § 115C-367

CROSS-DISTRICT Voluntary for districts. Requires approval of both resident district and receiving district. N.C. Gen. Stat. § 115C-366(d)

STATE LAWS CRIMINALIZING USE OF INCORRECT ADDRESS

N.C.Gen. Stat. § 115C-366(a3): If a student resides with a non-custodial adult, an affidavit must be submitted swearing that the student is not residing with that adult primarily to gain attendance at a particular school. If a person "willfully and knowingly provided false information in the affidavit, the maker of the affidavit shall be guilty of a Class 1 misdemeanor and shall pay to the local board an amount equal to the cost of educating the student during the period of enrollment."

CHARTER SCHOOL ADMISSIONS

Charter schools are forbidden from discriminating against students based on their residential address within the school district. The exception is conversion charter schools, which must give enrollment priority to students who reside in the former attendance area of the school. N.C.Gen. Stat. § 115C-218.45

NORTH DAKOTA

OPEN TO ALL?	Yes—*constitutional*
EQUAL EDUCATIONAL OPPORTUNITY?	No
FUNDAMENTAL RIGHT?	Yes—*Bismarck Public School District No. 1 v. State* (1994)

STATE CONSTITUTION

Art. 8 § 1. A high degree of intelligence, patriotism, integrity and morality on the part of every voter in a government by the people being necessary in order to insure the continuance of that government and the prosperity and happiness of the people, the legislative assembly shall make provision for the establishment and maintenance of a system of public schools which shall be open to all children of the state of North Dakota and free from sectarian control.

NOTES

In North Dakota, attendance zones could be vulnerable on two legal fronts: (1) a challenge based on the promise in the state constitution that the public schools be "open to all children of the state," and (2) an equal protection challenge with strict scrutiny review, because the ND Supreme Court has ruled education to be a fundamental right. The ND Supreme Court requires a supermajority of four justices (out of five total) to rule a statute unconstitutional.

STATE LAW ESTABLISHING ATTENDANCE ZONES

None found.

OPEN ENROLLMENT

WITHIN-DISTRICT No laws found. The largest district—Fargo Public Schools—has a policy (AP 6710) that allows students to attend schools outside their "assigned attendance area" but geographic enrollment preferences are in place for families in the zones.

CROSS-DISTRICT Voluntary for districts. It does not appear that the resident district must provide approval of transfer. N.D. Cent. Code § 15.1-31-06

STATE LAWS CRIMINALIZING USE OF INCORRECT ADDRESS

None found.

CHARTER SCHOOL ADMISSIONS

No charter school law.

SOUTH CAROLINA

OPEN TO ALL?	Yes— *constitutional*
EQUAL EDUCATIONAL OPPORTUNITY?	No
FUNDAMENTAL RIGHT?	No

STATE CONSTITUTION

Art. 11 § 3. The General Assembly shall provide for the maintenance and support of a system of free public schools open to all children in the State and shall establish, organize and support such other public institutions of learning, as may be desirable.

NOTES

In South Carolina, attendance zones could be vulnerable to a challenge based on the promise in the state constitution that the public schools be "open to all children in the State."

STATE LAW ESTABLISHING ATTENDANCE ZONES

None found.

OPEN ENROLLMENT

WITHIN-DISTRICT None found.
CROSS-DISTRICT Voluntary for districts. Resident district has veto power. S.C. Code § 59-63-490. Officials at receiving district can be fined or imprisoned if they accept a student without approval from the student's resident district. S.C. Code § 59-63-500

STATE LAWS CRIMINALIZING USE OF INCORRECT ADDRESS

S.C. Code § 59-63-32: "If it is found that a person wilfully and knowingly has provided false information in the affidavit provided for in subsection (B) to enroll a child in a school district for which the child is not eligible, the maker of the false affidavit is guilty of a misdemeanor and, upon conviction, must be fined an amount not to exceed two hundred dollars or imprisoned for not more than thirty days and also must be required to pay to the school district an amount equal to the cost to the district of educating the child during the period of enrollment. Repayment does not include funds paid by the State."

CHARTER SCHOOL ADMISSIONS

Charter schools are forbidden from discriminating against students based on their residential address. S.C. Code § 59-40-50

SOUTH DAKOTA

OPEN TO ALL? Yes— *constitutional*

EQUAL EDUCATIONAL OPPORTUNITY? No

FUNDAMENTAL RIGHT? No

STATE CONSTITUTION

Art. 8 § 1. The stability of a republican form of government depending on the morality and intelligence of the people, it shall be the duty of the Legislature to establish and maintain a general and uniform system of public schools wherein tuition shall be without charge, and equally open to all; and to adopt all suitable means to secure to the people the advantages and opportunities of education.

NOTES

In South Dakota, attendance zones could be vulnerable to a challenge based on the promise in the state constitution that the public schools be "equally open to all."

STATE LAW ESTABLISHING ATTENDANCE ZONES

S.D. Codified Laws § 13-28-19: "The school board shall assign and distribute the resident students eligible for elementary and secondary education among the schools in the district or to any public school in this state or any other state."

OPEN ENROLLMENT

WITHIN-DISTRICT Required for districts, but geographic enrollment preferences are allowed. S.D. Codified Laws § 13-28-44
CROSS-DISTRICT Required for districts, but geographic enrollment preferences allowed. S.D. Codified Laws § 13-28-21

STATE LAWS CRIMINALIZING USE OF INCORRECT ADDRESS

S.D. Codified Laws § 13-28-9: "The student or the student's parents or guardian may not establish school residence and be exempt from the payment of tuition if the residence of the parents or guardian of the student is acquired solely or principally for obtaining free school privileges."

CHARTER SCHOOL ADMISSIONS

No charter school law.

TENNESSEE

OPEN TO ALL?	No
EQUAL EDUCATIONAL OPPORTUNITY?	Yes—*TN Small School Systems v. McWherter* (1993)
FUNDAMENTAL RIGHT?	No

STATE CONSTITUTION

Art. 11 § 12. The state of Tennessee recognizes the inherent value of education and encourages its support. The General Assembly shall provide for the maintenance, support and eligibility standards of a system of free public schools. The General Assembly may establish and support such post-secondary educational institutions, including public institutions of higher learning, as it determines.

NOTES

In Tennessee, attendance zones could be vulnerable to a challenge based on the TN Supreme Court's ruling that the state constitution requires a school system that "affords substantially equal educational opportunities to all students."

STATE LAW ESTABLISHING ATTENDANCE ZONES

Tenn. Code § 49-6-3103: "In determining the particular public school to which pupils shall be assigned, the board of education may consider and base its decision on ... the geographical location of the place of residence of the pupil as related to the various schools of the system."

STATE LAWS CRIMINALIZING USE OF INCORRECT ADDRESS

None found.

CHARTER SCHOOL ADMISSIONS

No charter school law.

OPEN ENROLLMENT

WITHIN-DISTRICT Voluntary for districts. Tenn. Code § 49-6-3104(e): "Each local board of education may permit adult students or the parents or guardian of a minor student to choose the school the student is to attend. If the choice is for a school other than the one to which the student is normally zoned, the student may be required to provide personal transportation."

CROSS-DISTRICT Voluntary for districts. Transfers do not appear to require permission from the resident district. Tenn. Code § 49-6-3104(a).

VIRGINIA

OPEN TO ALL?	No
EQUAL EDUCATIONAL OPPORTUNITY?	No
FUNDAMENTAL RIGHT?	Yes—*Scott v. Virginia* (1994)

STATE CONSTITUTION

Art. 8 § 1. The General Assembly shall provide for a system of free public elementary and secondary schools for all children of school age throughout the Commonwealth, and shall seek to ensure that an educational program of high quality is established and continually maintained.

NOTES

In Virginia, attendance zones could be vulnerable to an equal protection challenge and strict scrutiny review, because the VA Supreme Court has ruled education to be a fundamental right.

STATE LAW ESTABLISHING ATTENDANCE ZONES

Va. Code § 22.1-79 states that school boards shall "provide for the consolidation of schools or redistricting of school boundaries or adopt pupil assignment plans whenever such procedure will contribute to the efficiency of the school division."

OPEN ENROLLMENT

WITHIN-DISTRICT Voluntary for districts. Va. Code § 22.1-7.1
CROSS-DISTRICT None found.

STATE LAWS CRIMINALIZING USE OF INCORRECT ADDRESS

Va. Code § 22.1-264.1: "Any person who knowingly makes a false statement concerning the residency of a child, as determined by § 22.1-3, in a particular school division or school attendance zone, for the purposes of (i) avoiding the tuition charges authorized by § 22.1-5 or (ii) enrollment in a school outside the attendance zone in which the student resides, shall be guilty of a Class 4 misdemeanor and shall be liable to the school division in which the child was enrolled as a result of such false statements for tuition charges, pursuant to § 22.1-5, for the time the student was enrolled in such school division."

CHARTER SCHOOL ADMISSIONS

Charter schools are forbidden from discriminating against students based on their residential address within the "school division," which is VA's term for a school district or jurisdiction. Va. Code § 22.1-212.6

WEST VIRGINIA

OPEN TO ALL?	No
EQUAL EDUCATIONAL OPPORTUNITY?	No
FUNDAMENTAL RIGHT?	Yes—*Pauley v. Kelly* (1979)

STATE CONSTITUTION

Art. 10 § 2. The Legislature shall provide, as soon as practicable, for the establishment of a thorough and efficient system of free schools.

NOTES

In West Virginia, attendance zones could be vulnerable to an equal protection challenge and strict scrutiny review, because the WV Supreme Court has ruled education to be a fundamental right.

STATE LAW ESTABLISHING ATTENDANCE ZONES

W.Va. Code § 18-5-16: "The county board may divide the county into such districts as are necessary to determine the schools the students of its county shall attend. Upon the written request of any parent or guardian, or person legally responsible for any student, or for reasons affecting the best interests of the schools, the superintendent may transfer students from one school to another within the county."

STATE LAWS CRIMINALIZING USE OF INCORRECT ADDRESS

None found.

CHARTER SCHOOL ADMISSIONS

West Virginia passed its first charter school law—House Bill 206—in the summer of 2019. The law allows charter schools to establish a "primary recruitment area" and to discriminate against children who live outside that area when making enrollment decisions.

OPEN ENROLLMENT

WITHIN-DISTRICT None found.
CROSS-DISTRICT Voluntary for districts. Resident district can veto the transfer. W.Va. Code § 18-5-16(b)

WISCONSIN

OPEN TO ALL?	No
EQUAL EDUCATIONAL OPPORTUNITY?	No
FUNDAMENTAL RIGHT?	Yes—*Kukor v. Grover* (1989)

STATE CONSTITUTION

Art. 10 § 3. The legislature shall provide by law for the establishment of district schools, which shall be as nearly uniform as practicable; and such schools shall be free and without charge for tuition to all children between the ages of 4 and 20 years....

NOTES

In Wisconsin, attendance zones could be vulnerable to an equal protection challenge and strict scrutiny review, because the WI Supreme Court has ruled "that it is a fundamental right of every child in this state to have an equal opportunity for education."

STATE LAW ESTABLISHING ATTENDANCE ZONES

None found.

STATE LAWS CRIMINALIZING USE OF INCORRECT ADDRESS

None found.

OPEN ENROLLMENT

WITHIN-DISTRICT Voluntary for districts. A school district may admit students outside of a school's attendance area prior to admitting students from outside the district. Wis. Stat. § 118.51
CROSS-DISTRICT Required for districts. But districts can refuse to enroll students if there is no space left over after residents of the district have been admitted. Wis. Stat. § 118.51

CHARTER SCHOOL ADMISSIONS

Charter schools are forbidden from discriminating against students based on their residential address within the school district. The exception is conversion charter schools that must give enrollment priority to students who reside in the former attendance area of the school. Wis. Stat. § 118.40

WYOMING

OPEN TO ALL?	No
EQUAL EDUCATIONAL OPPORTUNITY?	No
FUNDAMENTAL RIGHT?	Yes—*Washakie County School District v. Herschler* (1980)

STATE CONSTITUTION

Art. 7 § 1. The legislature shall provide for the establishment and maintenance of a complete and uniform system of public instruction, embracing free elementary schools of every needed kind and grade, a university with such technical and professional departments as the public good may require and the means of the state allow, and such other institutions as may be necessary.

NOTES

In Wyoming, attendance zones could be vulnerable to an equal protection challenge and strict scrutiny review, because the WY Supreme Court has ruled "the matter of education involves a fundamental interest of great public importance," which has been interpreted to mean that education is a fundamental right in Wyoming.

STATE LAW ESTABLISHING ATTENDANCE ZONES

None found.

STATE LAWS CRIMINALIZING USE OF INCORRECT ADDRESS

None found.

OPEN ENROLLMENT

WITHIN-DISTRICT None found.
CROSS-DISTRICT Voluntary for districts. Resident district cannot veto transfers. Wyo. Stat. § 21-4-502

CHARTER SCHOOL ADMISSIONS

Wyoming's charter school law does not prohibit charter schools from discriminating against students based on their residential address. Wyo. Stat. § 21-3-307 only specifies that a charter school application must contain "admission requirements, if applicable."

NOTES

Preface

1 Gloria Romero, "From Topeka, to Adelanto, and Montgomery County: Brown v. School Board of Education Continues—Taken from a Speech Given at Whittier Law School, April 9, 2013," *Whittier Journal of Child and Family Advocacy* 13 (2014): 20.

Chapter One

1 Minnesota Constitution of 1857, art. 8 § 1.
2 Arkansas Constitution of 1874, art. 14 § 1.
3 Florida Constitution of 1968, art. 9.
4 Horace Mann, *Life and Works of Horace Mann* (Boston, MA: Walker, Fuller and Company, 1868).
5 Serrano v. Priest, 487 P. 2d 1241 (CA Supreme Court 1971).
6 *Serrano v. Priest*, 487 P. 2d.
7 Ken Gormley, "Education as a Fundamental Right: Building a New Paradigm," *Forum on Public Policy (University of Illinois)* 2, no. 2 (2006): 207–29. Gormley identifies fourteen states where education has been ruled to be a "fundamental right." But the Tennessee court ruling in *Tennessee Small School Systems v. McWherter* (1993) explicitly declines to rule on whether education is a fundamental right and instead rules that the Tennessee constitution guarantees "substantially equal educational opportunities to all students."
8 Arizona Constitution of 1910, art. 11 § 6. South Carolina Constitution of 1895, art. XI § 3. Indiana Constitution of 1851, art. 8 § 1. Louisiana Constitution of 1974, art. 8 preamble. Montana Constitution of 1972, art. x § 1. North Carolina Constitution of 1971, art. 9 § 2.
9 Alabama Constitution of 1901, § 256.
10 Gary Kamiya, "How Early SF Kept Chinese Children out of the Schoolhouse," *San Francisco Chronicle*, April 15, 2017.
11 Brown v. Board of Education, 347 U.S. 483 (1954).

Chapter Two

1 "Family Urgent Care" and "Physicians Immediate Care - Old Town," Google Maps, accessed September 16, 2019.

2 Alan G. Artner, "Old Town," *Chicago Tribune*, March 29, 2008.

3 Chicago Public Schools, "CPS : Schools : Lincoln," accessed September 16, 2019, https://www.cps.edu/Schools/Pages/school.aspx?SchoolId=610038.

4 "About the School," Abraham Lincoln Elementary School, accessed September 16, 2019, http://www.lincolnelementary.org/about-the-school1.html.

5 Illinois State Board of Education, "Illinois Report Card," 2018, https://www.illinoisreportcard.com/.

6 Paul Biasco, "Lincoln Park School Annex Meeting Ends in Fist Fight," *DNAinfo Chicago* (blog), November 21, 2013, https://www.dnainfo.com/chicago/20131121/lincoln-park/lincoln-park-school-annex-meeting-ends-parent-fist-fight.

7 Chapter 105 Illinois Compiled Statutes § 10–21.3a (2009).

8 Ted Cox, "CTU Files Suit to Stop 10 School Closings, Citing Hearing Officers' Reports," *DNAinfo Chicago* (blog), May 29, 2013, https://www.dnainfo.com/chicago/20130529/chicago/ctu-files-suit-stop-10-school-closings-citing-hearing-officers-reports.

9 Mark Konkol and Paul Biasco, "Parents Win Battle, Manierre Elementary Won't Close," *My Chicago–DNAinfo Chicago* (blog), May 21, 2013, https://www.dnainfo.com/chicago/20130521/old-town/parents-win-battle-manierre-elementary-wont-close.

10 Matt Masterson, "CPS Space Utilization Data Shows More Underutilized Schools," WTTW News, accessed September 16, 2019, https://news.wttw.com/2018/12/31/cps-space-utilization-data-shows-more-underutilized-schools.

11 Sarah Carp, "Race 'Elephant in the Room' with Lincoln Overcrowding," *Chicago Reporter*, November 20, 2013.

12 Carp, "Race."

13 Chicago Public Schools, "CPS : Schools : Lincoln," accessed September 16, 2019, https://www.cps.edu/Schools/Pages/school.aspx?SchoolId=610038.

14 Chicago Public Schools, "CPS : Schools : Manierre," accessed September 16, 2019, https://cps.edu/Schools/Pages/school.aspx?SchoolID=610048.

15 Mary Schmich, "With Last-Minute Reprieve, School Gets Chance to Mend Divided Neighborhood," *Chicago Tribune*, May 24, 2013.

17 Eric Celeste, "Will APS Redistricting Destroy Candler Park?" *Creative Loafing*, February 23, 2012.

18 Keri Mitchell, "Dallas ISD Board Vote Pours Millions into East Dallas Schools," *Lakewood/East Dallas* (blog), March 27, 2015, https://lakewood.advocatemag.com/2015/03/27/dallas-isd-board-vote-pours-millions-into-east-dallas-schools/.

19 Los Angeles Unified School District, "About Us: Mount Washington Elementary School," accessed September 16, 2019, https://mtwashington-lausd-ca.schoolloop.com/about.

20 California Department of Education, "Smarter Balanced Results—CAASPP Reporting" for Mount Washington and Aragon Avenue Elementary Schools, 2019.

21 "School Profile: Mt. Washington Elementary (CA Dept of Education)," accessed September 16, 2019, https://www.cde.ca.gov/sdprofile/details.aspx?cds=19647336018246.

22 "School Profile: Aragon Avenue Elementary (CA Dept of Education)," accessed September 16, 2019, https://www.cde.ca.gov/sdprofile/details.aspx?cds=19647336015853.

23 Los Angeles Unified School District, "Policy Bulletin BUL-5347.1: Intra-District (School to School) Permits and Student Transfers in Elementary and Secondary Schools," April 1, 2016.

24 Kevin Gillen and Susan Wachter, "Neighborhood Value Updated: West Philadelphia Price Indexes" (University of Pennsylvania Institute for Urban Research, April 26, 2011), https://www.slideshare.net/PennUrbanResearch/neighborhood-value-updated-west-philadelphia-price-indexes.

25 Samantha Melamed, "The Penn Alexander Effect: Is There Any Room Left for Low-Income Residents in University City?" *Philadelphia Inquirer*, November 1, 2018.

26 Melamed, "Penn Alexander."

27 Mike Lyons, "In Catchment or Not, Penn Alexander Will Be Forced to Turn New Students Away," *West Philly Local*, parent comment by "Linda," May 11, 2011.

28 Lyons, "In Catchment," parent comment by "missy," May 11, 2011.

29 Lyons, "In Catchment," parent comment by "Anon," May 11, 2011.

30 Lyons, "In Catchment," parent comment by "Suzanne," May 11, 2011.

31 Mike Lyons, "Follow Up: Questions Arise after Penn Alexander Catchment Story," *West Philly Local*, parent comment by "Liz," May 12, 2011.

32 Lyons, "In Catchment," parent comment by "Chris," May 11, 2011.

Chapter Three

1 Federal Housing Administration, *Underwriting Manual: Underwriting and Valuation Procedure under Title II of the National Housing Act with Revisions to February, 1938, Part II, Section 9, Rating of Location*, 1938.

2 Tracy Jan, "Redlining Was Banned 50 Years Ago. It's Still Hurting Minorities Today," *Washington Post*, March 28, 2018.

3 Dana Wilkie, "Governor OKs Bills on Choice of Schools," *San Diego Union-Tribune*, July 23, 1993.

4 Open Enrollment Act, California Education Code § 35160.5 (1993).

5 Maria Newman, "California Schools Vying for New Students under a State Plan for Open Enrollments," *New York Times*, May 25, 1994.

6 Open Enrollment Act.

7 Los Angeles Unified School District, "Policy Bulletin BUL-6491.1: District's K–12 Open Enrollment Transfers for Elementary and Secondary Students," April 1, 2016.

8 Los Angeles Unified School District, "Understanding the Open Enrollment Declaration," 2019.

9 Los Angeles Unified School District, "2018–2019 Open Enrollment Transfers Verification," 2018.

10 Tanya Anton, "Re: Possible School Workshop in Highland Park," email message to author, January 3, 2019.

11 California Department of Education Data Reporting Office, "K–12 Public School Enrollment, 6058135-Mark Twain Middle, Time Series - Public School Enrollment," accessed September 16, 2019, https://dq.cde.ca.gov/dataquest/DQ/EnrTimeRptSch.aspx?cYear=2007-08&Level=School&cName=Mark+Twain+Middle&cCode=6058135&dCode=1964733.

12 National Center for Education Statistics, "Digest of Education Statistics, 2017. Table 206.30. Percentage of Students Enrolled in Grades 1 through 12, by Public School Type and Charter Status, Private School Type, and Selected Child and Household Characteristics: 2016," 2019.

13 Ohio Revised Code § 3319.01.

14 Pennsylvania Public School Code of 1949 § 1310.

15 Richard Rothstein, *The Color of Law: A Forgotten History of How Our Government Segregated America* (New York: Liveright Publishing, 2017).

16 Terry Gross, "A 'Forgotten History' of How the U.S. Government Segregated America," *Fresh Air*, NPR, May 3, 2017.

17 Bruce Mitchell and Juan Franco, "HOLC 'Redlining' Maps: The Persistent Structure of Segregation and Economic Inequality" (Washington, DC: National Community Reinvestment Coalition, 2016).

18 Tracy Jan, "Redlining."

19 Los Angeles Unified School District Master Planning and Demographics Facilities Services Division, "Ivanhoe Elementary School Attendance Area," 2007.

20 California Department of Education, "Enrollment by Ethnicity: Ivanhoe Elementary," accessed November 12, 2019, https://dq.cde.ca.gov/dataquest/dqcensus/enrethlevels.aspx?agglevel=School&year=2018–19&cds=19647336017685.

21 Salvatore Saporito and David Van Riper, "Do Irregularly Shaped School Attendance Zones Contribute to Racial Segregation or Integration?" *Social Currents* 3, no. 1 (March 1, 2016): 64–83, https://doi.org/10.1177/2329496515604637.

22 Meredith Richards, "Gerrymandering Educational Opportunity," *Phi Delta Kappan*, November 13, 2017.

23 Birmingham City Schools, "2019–2020 Zone and Feeder Pattern," April 23, 2019.

24 Meyer Weinberg, *Race & Place: A Legal History of the Neighborhood School* (U.S. Department of Health, Education, and Welfare Office of Education, 1967).

25 Jim Epstein, "Brownstone Brooklyn's Racial Divide: Why Are the Schools So Segregated?," *ReasonTV*, January 27, 2016, https://www.youtube.com/watch?v=yePxe4kKC5k.

26 Virginia Walden Ford, "School Choice the Fastest Track to Integration," *The Hill*, May 23, 2017, https://thehill.com/blogs/pundits-blog/education/334608-school-choice-the-fastest-track-to-integration.

Chapter Four

1 Interview with Tom and Jennifer DeRoche, December 5, 2018.

2 Wisconsin Department of Public Instruction, "Accountability Report Cards," 2018, https://apps2.dpi.wi.gov/reportcards/home.

3 Illinois State Board of Education, "Illinois Report Card," 2018, https://www.illinoisreportcard.com/.

4 Wisconsin Department of Public Instruction, "Accountability Report Cards," 2018.

5 Genevieve Siegel-Hawley, *When the Fences Come Down: Twenty-First-Century Lessons from Metropolitan School Desegregation* (Chapel Hill, NC: University of North Carolina Press, 2016).

6 Mary Anne Brush, "The Last First Day," *Grosse Pointe News*, September 4, 2019.

7 Mary Anne Brush, "Maire Parents Look to the Facts," *Grosse Pointe News*, June 5, 2019.

8 Grosse Pointe Public School System, "Mandatory Residency Verification," accessed September 18, 2019, https://mi01000971.schoolwires.net/Page/17866.

9 Grosse Pointe Public School System, "Enrollment Eligibility Investigations," accessed September 18, 2019, https://mi01000971.schoolwires.net/Page/1042.

10 Christian Barnard, "Some People Are Buying Their Way Into Top Public Schools. That's Not How School Choice Should Work," *Reason*, June 21, 2019.

11 Micah Ann Wixom and Tom Keily, "50-State Comparison: Open Enrollment Policies" (Education Commission of the States, October 30, 2018).

12 June Kronholz, "California's Districts of Choice: Superintendents Compete for Students," *Education Next* 14, no. 3 (Summer 2014): 38–45.

13 California Department of Education, "2018–19 Districts of Choice," October 2018, https://www.cde.ca.gov/sp/eo/dc/index.asp.

14 "Pupil Attendance Alternatives," California Education Code § 48301 (2009).

15 Jim Weiker and Mark Ferenchik, "Program to Move 100 Low-Income Columbus Families to Suburban School Districts," *Columbus Dispatch*, May 1, 2017.

16 Ohio Department of Education Office of Quality School Choice and Funding, "Open Enrollment Report for the 2018/2019 School Year," December 2018, http://education.ohio.gov/Topics/Ohio-Education-Options/Open-Enrollment.

17 Rebecca Sibilia, Zahava Stadler, and Sara Hodges, "Fractured: The Accelerating Breakdown of America's School Districts, 2019 Update" (EdBuild, April 2019).

18 Lauren Camera, "The Quiet Wave of School District Secessions," *US News & World Report*, May 5, 2017.

19 Sibilia, "Fractured."

20 Kendra Bischoff, "School District Fragmentation and Racial Residential Segregation: How Do Boundaries Matter?" *Urban Affairs Review* 44, no. 2 (November 2008): 182–217.

21 Jennifer B. Ayscue and Gary Orfield, "School District Lines Stratify Educational Opportunity by Race and Poverty," *Race and Social Problems* 7, no. 1 (March 1, 2015): 5–20.

22 Jon Shure, "End New Jersey's Fragmentation," *City Belt*, February 25, 2007.

23 Bischoff, "School District Fragmentation."

24 Valencia Stovall, HB 788 (2018), http://www.legis.ga.gov/legislation/en-US/Display/20172018/HB/788.

25 Interview with Rep. Valencia Stovall (D - Forest Park) of the Georgia House of Representatives, December 21, 2018.

Chapter Five

1 Interview with Heather Yang (not her real name), October 9, 2018.

2 Michelle Higgins, "Your Address, as Get-Into-School Card," *New York Times*, May 3, 2013.

3 New York State Education Department, "New York State School Report Card - PS 87 William Sherman," August 22, 2018.

4 New York State Education Department, "New York State School Report Card - PS 153 Adam Clayton Powell," August 22, 2018.

5 Interview with Amanda Turner (not her real name), December 6, 2018.

6 Interview with Lakisha Young, October 9, 2018.

7 California Department of Education, "Smarter Balanced Results—CAASPP Reporting" for Peralta Elementary School, 2018.

8 California Department of Education, "Smarter Balanced Results—CAASPP Reporting" for Sankofa Academy, 2018.

9 Timothy Williams, "Jailed for Switching Her Daughters' School District," *New York Times*, September 26, 2011.

10 Jeff St. Clair, "The 'Rosa Parks Moment' for Education?" *All Things Considered*, NPR, January 28, 2011.

11 Neal Conan, "Parents Cross Lines to Get Kids Into Good Schools," *Talk of the Nation*, NPR, January 26, 2011.

12 Brad Segall, "Phila. Father Pleads Guilty to Falsely Enrolling Daughter in Suburban School," January 28, 2014, *CBS, Philadelphia*.

13 Jessica Spies, "Rochester Mom Gets Probation for Lying about Residence," *Daily Messenger*, MPNnow, July 29, 2019, https://www.mpnnow.com/article/20090729/NEWS/307299847.

14 Joseph Williams, "Despite Fines and Prison Time, Parents Keep Jumping School Boundaries for a Quality Education," *TakePart* (blog), December 5, 2014, http://www.takepart.com/article/2014/12/05/despite-fines-prison-time-parents-hopping-school-boundaries.

15 Interview with Jeff Bedford (not his real name), November 14, 2018.

16 Interview with Mo and Manijeh Naficy, December 8, 2018.

17 California Department of Education, "Smarter Balanced Results—CAASPP Reporting" for Birmingham and Reseda High Schools, 2018.

Chapter Six

1 Interview with Grace Lee Sawin of Chicago School GPS, December 5, 2018.

2 National Center for Education Statistics, "Digest of Education Statistics, 2017. Tables 206.20 and 206.40," January 2019.

3 National Center for Education Statistics, "Digest of Education Statistics, 2017."

4 National Center for Education Statistics, "Digest of Education Statistics, 2017."

5 Alissa Quart, "Here Come the Public-School Consultants," *Atlantic*, December 8, 2015.

6 Interview with Robin Aronow of School Search NYC, November 29, 2018.

7 Alina Adams, "How It Really Works: Behind the Scenes of a NYC Public School Waitlist & More Parent Portal Glitches!" *New York School Talk* (blog), April 8, 2019, http://newyorkschooltalk.org/2019/04/really-works-behind-scenes-nyc-public-school-waitlist-parent-portal-glitches/.

8 National Center for Education Statistics, "Digest of Education Statistics, 2017. Table 204.90," January 2019.

9 Jason A. Grissom and Christopher Redding, "Discretion and Disproportionality: Explaining the Underrepresentation of High-Achieving Students of Color in Gifted Programs," *AERA Open* 2, no. 1 (2016), https://doi.org/10.1177/2332858415622175.

10 Michelle Luce, "Parents Increasingly Using School Consultants to Steer Kids," *Education News* (blog), December 1, 2011, https://www.educationnews.org/parenting/parents-increasingly-using-school-consultants-to-steer-kids/.

11 Interview with Tanya Anton of the GoMama Guide, October 19, 2018.

12 Mike Lyons, "Follow Up: Questions Arise after Penn Alexander Catchment Story," *West Philly Local*, Parent comment by "Liz," May 12, 2011.

13 Mike Lyons, "In Catchment or Not, Penn Alexander Will Be Forced to Turn New Students Away," *West Philly Local*, Parent comment by "Chris," May 11, 2011.

14 Lyons, "In Catchment."

15 Sandra E. Black, "Do Better Schools Matter? Parental Valuation of Elementary Education," *Quarterly Journal of Economics* 114, no. 2 (May 1, 1999): 577–99.

16 Abbigail Chiodo, Rubén Hernández-Murillo, and Michael T. Owyang, "Nonlinear Effects of School Quality on House Prices," *Federal Reserve Bank of St. Louis Review* 92, no. 3 (May/June 2010).

17 Jacqueline Tager, "Update," email message to author, May 18, 2019.

18 Lisa Rantala, "Living Outside District Lines," *ABC6 News* (Columbus, Ohio: WSYX), August 17, 2018.

19 San Francisco Unified School District, "SFUSD: Enrollment Policies," accessed September 19, 2019, https://archive.sfusd.edu/en/enroll-in-sfusd-schools/policy-reference.html.

20 Carla Rivera, "All Beverly Hills Students Soon May Be Required to Prove Their Residency," *Los Angeles Times*, January 17, 2010.

21 Laura Coleman, "Beverly Hills News – BHUSD to Crack Down on Students Living out of City," *Beverly Hills Courier* (blog), August 15, 2014, https://bhcourier.com/2014/08/14/beverly-hills-news-bhusd-crack-students-living-city/.

22 Beverly Hills Unified School District, "2018–19 Adopted Budget," June 19, 2018, https://www.bhusd.org/apps/pages/index.jsp?uREC_ID=31867&type=d&pREC_ID=175462.

23 Nicholas Schuler, *Annual Report, FY2018*, Office of the Inspector General of the Chicago Public Schools (January 1, 2019).

24 Mitchell Armentrout, "CPS Watchdog Found Some CPS Employees Cheated to Get Children into Top Schools," *Chicago Sun-Times*, January 3, 2019.

25 Philip A. Becnel IV, "Investigating Residency Fraud," *Fraud Magazine*, August 2014, https://www.fraud-magazine.com/article.aspx?id=4294984805.

26 Martinez v. Bynum, 461 U.S. 321 (1983).

27 Stephen Ceasar, "L.A. Charter School Aims to Toss Out Students with Fake Addresses," *Los Angeles Times*, March 12, 2013.

28 Ceasar, "L.A. Charter School."

29 Interview with Melissa (not her real name), June 9, 2019.

Chapter Seven

1 Nikole Hannah-Jones, "Choosing a School for My Daughter in a Segregated City," *New York Times Magazine*, June 9, 2016.

2 Alex Zimmerman, "Fariña to Parents: We Need 'Organic' Plans, Not Mandates, to Diversify Schools," *Chalkbeat* (blog), February 24, 2016, https://www.chalkbeat.org/posts/ny/2016/02/24/farina-to-parents-we-need-organic-plans-not-mandates-to-diversify-schools/.

3 "De Blasio Is Trying to Kill NYC's Charter Schools," *New York Post*, May 3, 2018, https://nypost.com/2018/05/03/de-blasio-is-trying-to-kill-nycs-charter-schools/.

4 Julia Marsh, "De Blasio Shouts That He 'Hates' Charter Schools at Campaign Event," July 20, 2019, https://nypost.com/2019/07/08/de-blasio-shouts-that-he-hates-charter -schools-at-campaign-event/.

5 Sara Feijo, "Here's What Happened When Boston Tried to Assign Students Good Schools Close to Home," *News@Northeastern* (blog), July 26, 2018, https://news .northeastern.edu/2018/07/16/heres-what-happened-when-boston-tried-to-assign -students-good-schools-close-to-home/.

6 Chris Hammond, "Parents Cross Their Fingers in Berkeley School Lottery," *Berkeleyside* (blog), February 4, 2011, https://www.berkeleyside.com/2011/02/04/parents-cross -their-fingers-in-berkeley-school-lottery.

7 Mark Byrnes, "Buffalo Was Once a Model for Integration. Now the Vast Majority of Its Public Schools Are Segregated," *CityLab* (blog), April 11, 2014, https://www .citylab.com/equity/2014/04/how-buffalos-once-diverse-schools-became-some-most -segregated/8823/.

8 Alejandra Matos, "This Is How the D.C. School Lottery Is Supposed to Work," *Washington Post*, May 27, 2017.

9 Jacqueline Rabe Thomas, "Is School Choice Really a Choice, or a Chance?" *Hartford Courant*, September 10, 2015.

10 Jessica Williams, "A Third of New Orleans Students Don't Get into One of Their Top 3 Schools of Choice," *New Orleans Advocate*, April 16, 2018.

11 Katrina Schwartz, "How the San Francisco School Lottery Works, and How It Doesn't," *Bay Curious*, KQED, (January 11, 2018).

12 Perry Stein, Peter Jamison, and Fenit Nirappil, "D.C. Public Schools Leader to Resign after Skirting School Assignment Rules, *Washington Post*, February 20, 2018.

13 Williams, "Third of New Orleans Students."

14 Allison McCann, "When School Choice Means Choosing Segregation," *Vice* (blog), April 12, 2017, https://www.vice.com/en_us/article/j5d3q3/when-school-choice -means-choosing-segregation.

15 Erin Aubry Kaplan, "School Choice Is the Enemy of Justice," *New York Times*, August 14, 2018.

16 Erica Frankenberg, Genevieve Siegel-Hawley, Jia Wang, and Gary Orfield, "Choice without Equity: Charter School Segregation and the Need for Civil Rights Standards," June 26, 2012, https://escholarship.org/uc/item/4r07q8kg.

17 "Establishment of Charter Schools," California Education Code § 47605(b)(5)(G) (1993).

18 National Center for Education Statistics, "Digest of Education Statistics, 2017."

19 Tomas Monarrez, Brian Kisida, and Matthew M. Chingos, "Do Charter Schools Increase Segregation? First National Analysis Reveals a Modest Impact, Depending on Where You Look," *Education Next* 19, no. 4 (Fall 2019).

20 Monarrez, Kisida, and Chingos, "Do Charter Schools."

21 Interview with Tanya Anton of the GoMama Guide, October 19, 2018.

Chapter Eight

1 Bob Herman, "Earnings of Health Care Companies Have Soared under the ACA," *Axios* (blog), October 18, 2018, https://www.axios.com/aca-health-care-industry -insurance-hospitals-profit-856273fc-4248-4021-adf3-dfda8bc13040.html.

2 Stuart Buck and Bruce Yandle, "Bootleggers, Baptists, and the Global Warming Battle," SSRN Scholarly Paper (Rochester, NY: Social Science Research Network, August 14, 2001), https://papers.ssrn.com/abstract=279914.

3 California Commission for the Review of the Master Plan for Higher Education, "The Master Plan Renewed: Unity, Equity, Quality, and Efficiency in California Postsecondary Education," 1987.

4 "Community Colleges, Education Programs, Interdistrict Attendance," California Education Code § 78030 (1987).

5 National Center for Education Statistics, "Digest of Education Statistics, 2017. Table 203.20," January 2019.

6 Community Reinvestment Act, 12 U.S.C. § 2901 (1977).

7 Plyler v. Doe, 457 U.S. 202 (1982).

8 United States v. Virginia, 518 U.S. 515 (1996).

Chapter Nine

1 John Eastman, "Reinterpreting the Education Clauses in State Constitutions," in *School Money Trials: The Legal Pursuit of Educational Adequacy*, ed. Martin R. West and Paul E. Peterson, 55–74 (Brookings Institution Press, 2007).

2 Jackson v. Pasadena City School District, 59 Cal. 2d 876 (CA Supreme Court 1971).

3 Serrano v. Priest, 487 P. 2d 1241 (CA Supreme Court 1971).

4 San Antonio Independent School District v. Rodriguez, 411 U.S. 1 (1973).

5 Campaign for Fiscal Equity v. State of New York, 86 2d 307 (N.Y. Court of Appeals 1995).

6 Rose v. Council for Better Education, *Inc.,* Kentucky Supreme Court, 790 S.W.2d 186 (K.Y. Supreme Court 1989).

7 Vergara v. State of California, 246 Cal. App. 4th 619 (Court of Appeal, 2nd Appellate Dist., 2nd Div. 2016).

8 Sonali Kohli, "What the Vergara Ruling Means for the Future of Teacher Tenure in the U.S.," *Los Angeles Times*, April 15, 2016, https://www.latimes.com/local/education/la-me-edu-vergara-future-20160414-snap-htmlstory.html.

9 Christopher Magan, "Minnesota Appeals Court Blocks Lawsuit over Teacher Tenure, Again," *Twin Cities Pioneer Press*, January 22, 2019.

10 Eastman, "Reinterpreting."

11 Baker v. Carr, 369 U.S. 186 (162AD).

12 Tennessee Small School Systems v. McWherter, 851 S.W.2d 139 (Tennessee Supreme Court 1993).

13 810 Ill. Comp. Stat. § 5/10-21.3 (1963).

14 Milliken v. Bradley, 418 U.S. 717 (1974).

Chapter Ten

1 Stephen Middleton, *The Black Laws: Race and the Legal Process in Early Ohio* (Athens Ohio: Ohio University Press, 2005).

2 Horace Mann, *Life and Works of Horace Mann* (Boston, MA: Walker, Fuller and Company, 1868).

3 Brown v. Board of Education, 347 U.S. 483 (1954).

4 Milliken v. Bradley, 418 U.S. 717 (1974).

5 San Antonio Independent School District v. Rodriguez, 411 U.S. 1 (1973).

6 Plyler v. Doe, 457 U.S. 202 (1982).

7 Martinez v. Bynum, 461 U.S. 321 (1983).

8 Parents Involved in Community Schools v. Seattle School Dist. No. 1, 551 U.S. 701 (2007).

9 810 Ill. Comp. Stat. § 5/10–21.3 (1963).

10 Chicago Public Schools, "Chicago Public Schools Policy Manual, Section 702.1 Enrollment and Transfer of Students in the Chicago Public Schools," April 26, 2017.

11 *San Antonio Independent School District v. Rodriguez.*

12 F. S. Royster Guano v. Virginia, 253 U.S. 412 (1920).

13 Reed v. Reed, 404 U.S. 71 (1971).

14 Craig v. Boren, 429 U.S. 190 (1976).

15 *Craig v. Boren.*

16 J.E.B. v. Alabama ex rel. T.B., 511 U.S. 127 (1994).

17 Weber v. Aetna Cas. & Sur. Co., 406 U.S. 164 (1972).

18 City of Cleburne v. Cleburne Living Center, *Inc.*, 473 U.S. 432 (1985).

19 United States v. O'Brien, 391 U.S. 367 (1968).

20 Renton v. Playtime Theatres, Inc., 475 U.S. 41 (1986).

21 United States v. Virginia, 518 U.S. 515 (1996).

22 Sweatt v. Painter, 339 U.S. 629 (1950).

23 Plyler v. Doe.

24 *Parents Involved in Community Schools v. Seattle School Dist. No. 1.*

Chapter Eleven

1 Equal Educational Opportunities Act, 20 U.S.C. § 1701-1758 (1974).

2 Domenico Montanaro, "Biden Supported a Constitutional Amendment to End Mandated Busing in 1975," *NPR.org* (blog), June 28, 2019, https://www.npr .org/2019/06/28/736995314/listen-biden-supported-a-constitutional-amendment-to -end-mandated-busing-in-1975.

3 "Transcript of Nixon's Statement on School Busing," *New York Times*, March 17, 1972.

4 Equal Educational Opportunities Act.

5 Flores v. Arizona, 516 F.3d 1140 (2008).

Chapter Twelve

1 Alexandria Ocasio-Cortez, Twitter post, July 1, 2018, https://twitter.com/aoc /status/1013480623531593735.

2 Brown v. Board of Education, 347 U.S. 483 (1954).

3 Malcolm Gladwell, "Miss Buchanan's Period of Adjustment," *Revisionist History*, podcast, June 28, 2017, http://revisionisthistory.com/episodes/13-miss-buchanans -period-of-adjustment. Leola Brown quotation is from an oral history of the Kansas State Historical Society.

4 Freeman v. Pitts, 503 U.S. 467 (1992).

5 Swann v. Charlotte-Mecklenburg Board of Education, 402 U.S. 1 (1971).
6 Board of Education of Oklahoma City v. Dowell, 498 U.S. 237 (1991).

Appendix A

1 Eric Celeste, "Will APS Redistricting Destroy Candler Park?," *Creative Loafing*, February 23, 2012, https://creativeloafing.com/content-185613-cover-story-will-aps-redistricting-destroy-candler.

2 Celeste, "Will APS Redistricting."

3 David Terraso, "Mary Lin Opens New Building and Outdoor Classroom," *Candler Park Messenger*, August 2015.

4 Phone call to office of Mary Lin Elementary School, August 27, 2019.

5 Phone call to the School Choice Division of the Columbus CitySchools, August 28, 2019.

6 Keri Mitchell, "Mata Montessori Next Fall: Another Choice for East Dallas Parents?," *Lakewood/East Dallas* (blog), April 9, 2014, https://lakewood.advocatemag.com/2014/04/09/mata-montessori-next-fall-another-choice-east-dallas-parents/.

7 Keri Mitchell, "Dallas ISD Board Vote Pours Millions into East Dallas Schools," *Lakewood/East Dallas* (blog), March 27, 2015, https://lakewood.advocatemag.com/2015/03/27/dallas-isd-board-vote-pours-millions-into-east-dallas-schools/.

8 "Choice and Enrollment," Denver Public Schools, accessed September 5, 2019, http://schoolchoice.dpsk12.org/.

9 Phone call to office of Cory Elementary School, August 28, 2019.

10 Broward County Public Schools, "School Counseling & BRACE Advisement / Register My Child," accessed September 3, 2019, https://www.browardschools.com/register-for-school.

11 "Policy 5.1 Enrollment and Withdrawal" (2016), https://www.browardschools.com/cms/lib/FL01803656/Centricity/domain/13519/documents/Policy%205.1.pdf.

12 Stephanie Wang, "Why This IPS School Is Mostly White and Wealthy," *Indianapolis Star,* July 2, 2016.

13 Phone call to office of Center for Inquiry 84, August 28, 2019.

14 Topher Sanders, "Duval County Parents Squabble over Policy for Spots at Magnet School," *Florida Times-Union,* April 26, 2011.

15 Carianne Luter, "Jason Mraz Surprises Jacksonville Students with Performance," *News4Jax* (Jacksonville FL: WJXT), August 20, 2018.

16 Jim Piggott and Francine Frazier, "Parents Say Deadly Shootings Highlight Dangers at Some City Parks," WJXT, February 15, 2019.

17 Phone call to office of Hendricks Avenue Elementary School, August 27, 2019.

18 Tanya Anton, "School Boundary Changes – It Can Happen," GoMamaGuide (blog), June 4, 2015, https://gomamaguide.com/tag/moving-into-a-school-district/.

19 Phone call to office of Canfield Avenue Elementary School, August 27, 2019.

20 Jim Epstein, "Brownstone Brooklyn's Racial Divide: Why Are the Schools So Segregated?" *ReasonTV,* January 27, 2016, https://www.youtube.com/watch?v=yePxe4kKC5k.

21 Phone call to office of PS 8 Robert Fulton, August 29, 2019.

22 Kate Taylor, "Rezoning Plan for Manhattan Elementary School Draws Anger From All Sides," *New York Times,* September 29, 2016.

23 "No to Re-Zoning Lincoln Towers from PS 199 to PS 191," Change.org, accessed September 6, 2019, https://www.change.org/p/cec3-no-to-re-zoning-lincoln-towers -from-ps-199-to-ps-191.

24 Kate Taylor, "Upper West Side School Zones Changed, but Not All Parents Went Along," *New York Times,* November 10, 2017.

25 "Meeting Notes of the Peralta Parent-Teacher Group Town Hall July 17, 2019," Peralta Elementary, accessed September 10, 2019, https://www.peraltaschool.org/pptg -minutes/2017/11/8/nov-1-2017-pptg-meeting-notes-6d5sk.

26 Ali Tadayon, "Oakland Parents Push Back against Plan to Close School," *East Bay Times,* July 15, 2019.

27 Phone call to office of Chesterton Elementary School, August 26, 2019.

28 Maureen Magee, "SD Schools Adopt STEAM Focus to Boost Enrollment, Meet Demand," *San Diego Union-Tribune,* September 30, 2016.

29 Phone call to office of James F. Smith Elementary School, August 27, 2019.

30 Phone call to office of John Hay Elementary School, August 27, 2019.

BIBLIOGRAPHY

Ayscue, Jennifer B., and Gary Orfield. "School District Lines Stratify
    Educational Opportunity by Race and Poverty." *Race and
    Social Problems* 7, no. 1 (March 1, 2015): 5–20.

Becnel, Philip A., IV. "Investigating Residency Fraud." *Fraud Magazine*,
    August 2014.

Bischoff, Kendra. "School District Fragmentation and Racial
    Residential Segregation: How Do Boundaries Matter?" *Urban
    Affairs Review* 44, no. 2 (November 2008): 182–217.

Black, Sandra E. "Do Better Schools Matter? Parental Valuation of
    Elementary Education." *Quarterly Journal of Economics* 114, no.
    2 (May 1, 1999): 577–99.

Bolick, Clint. *Unfinished Business: A Civil Rights Strategy for America's
    Third Century.* Berkeley, CA: Pacific Research Institute for
    Public Policy, 1990.

Buck, Stuart, and Bruce Yandle. "Bootleggers, Baptists, and the Global
    Warming Battle," August 14, 2001. https://papers.ssrn.com/
    abstract=279914.

Chiodo, Abbigail, Rubén Hernández-Murillo, and Michael T.
    Owyang. "Nonlinear Effects of School Quality on House
    Prices." *Federal Reserve Bank of St. Louis Review* 92, no. May/
    June 2010.

Eastman, John. "Reinterpreting the Education Clauses in State Constitutions." In *School Money Trials: The Legal Pursuit of Educational Adequacy*, edited by Martin R. West and Paul E. Peterson, 55–74. Washington, DC: Brookings Institution Press, 2007.

Frankenberg, Erica, Genevieve Siegel-Hawley, Jia Wang, and Gary Orfield. "Choice without Equity: Charter School Segregation and the Need for Civil Rights Standards," June 26, 2012. https://escholarship.org/uc/item/4r07q8kg.

Gillen, Kevin, and Susan Wachter. "Neighborhood Value Updated: West Philadelphia Price Indexes." University of Pennsylvania Institute for Urban Research, April 26, 2011.

Gormley, Ken. "Education as a Fundamental Right: Building a New Paradigm." *Forum on Public Policy* 2, no. 2 (2006): 207–29.

Hannah-Jones, Nikole. "Choosing a School for My Daughter in a Segregated City." *New York Times Magazine*, June 9, 2016.

Kronholz, June. "California's Districts of Choice: Superintendents Compete for Students." *Education Next* 14, no. 3 (Summer 2014): 38–45.

Mann, Horace. *Life and Works of Horace Mann*. Boston, MA: Walker, Fuller and Company, 1868.

Middleton, Stephen. *The Black Laws: Race and the Legal Process in Early Ohio*. Athens, OH: Ohio University Press, 2005.

Mitchell, Bruce, and Juan Franco. "HOLC 'Redlining' Maps: The Persistent Structure of Segregation and Economic Inequality." Washington, DC: National Community Reinvestment Coalition, 2016.

Quart, Alissa. "Here Come the Public-School Consultants." *Atlantic*, December 8, 2015.

Richards, Meredith. "Gerrymandering Educational Opportunity." *Phi Delta Kappan*, November 13, 2017.

Romero, Gloria. "From Topeka, to Adelanto, and Montgomery County: *Brown v. School Board of Education* Continues—Taken from a Speech Given at Whittier Law School, April 9, 2013." *Whittier Journal of Child and Family Advocacy* 13 (2014): 20.

Root, Damon. *Overruled: The Long War for Control of the US Supreme Court.* New York, NY: Palgrave Macmillan, 2014.

Rothstein, Richard. *The Color of Law: A Forgotten History of How Our Government Segregated America.* New York: Liveright Publishing, 2017.

Saporito, Salvatore, and David Van Riper. "Do Irregularly Shaped School Attendance Zones Contribute to Racial Segregation or Integration?" *Social Currents* 3, no. 1 (March 1, 2016): 64–83.

Shure, Jon. "Ending New Jersey's Fragmentation." *City Belt*, February 25, 2007.

Sibilia, Rebecca, Zahava Stadler, and Sara Hodges. "Fractured: The Accelerating Breakdown of America's School Districts, 2019 Update." EdBuild, April 2019.

Siegel-Hawley, Genevieve. *When the Fences Come Down: Twenty-First-Century Lessons from Metropolitan School Desegregation.* Chapel Hill, NC: University of North Carolina Press Books, 2016.

Weinberg, Meyer. *Race & Place: A Legal History of the Neighborhood School.* US Department of Health, Education, and Welfare Office of Education, 1967.

West, Martin R., and Paul E. Peterson. *School Money Trials: The Legal Pursuit of Educational Adequacy.* Washington, DC: Brookings Institution Press, 2007.

Wixom, Micah Ann, and Tom Keily. "50-State Comparison: Open Enrollment Policies." Education Commission of the States, October 30, 2018.

INDEX

Figures between pages 64 and 65 are referenced by *64fig* followed by the figure number. Notes are indicated by *n* following the page number.

ACKNOWLEDGMENTS

Gloria Romero was the inspiration for this book. She tells the truth and does what's right for kids, no matter the political price. And she retains her sense of humor. I'm honored to call her a friend.

I am also deeply indebted to my friend Jill Stewart, the former managing editor of the *LA Weekly*, for serving as my editor and bringing out the best in this manuscript. She was the perfect fit for this book, bringing passion, a keen ear for the language, and the instincts of a top-notch journalist.

Daniel González is a gifted designer and a true friend. He did brilliant work on the maps in this book, and they tell a story that is impossible to capture in words.

Kirsten Johnson served not only as a researcher but as a thought partner too. She brought diligence and rigor to the task, and she worked with a speed that was hard to believe. She made a huge contribution to both of the appendices. Sally Dworsky helped with the analysis of open enrollment seats in Los Angeles. Andreanna Ditton did a bit of important research that turned me on to the Equal Educational Opportunities Act.

Michele Jones copyedited the book, and Sarah Johansson was our proofreader. Maria Sosnowski indexed the book. All three made significant contributions to the work.

I owe a special debt to those scholars who provided invaluable feedback on the legal and policy issues raised in the book: Anthony Sanders at the Institute for Justice, John Eastman at Chapman University, and Josh Dunn at the University of Colorado Colorado Springs. I am also grateful to the friends who read early drafts of the book and were honest with me about its shortcomings: Jason Mandell, J. B. Waterman, Christine Sowder, and Laura DeRoche.

I also want to offer a special *thank you* to all the parents who shared their stories with me. Our education system creates all sorts of barriers for American families, and I admire the moms and dads who are willing to surmount those barriers in pursuit of opportunity for their kids.

Finally, thanks to my family—Simone, Neve, and Orik—for giving me a powerful motivation to finish this book so that I could get back to spending my free time with them.